PRAISE FOR *THE UNLOCKED LEADER*

"Hortense le Gentil writes the way she lives—authentically. The inspiration her new book provides about being a human leader speaks to me personally. For over fifty years I have tried to lead my company not as distant employees, but as family seeking success through shared values. I have tried to lead through empathy, sharing values that respect each of us as individuals. Hortense shares with us ways to unlock the humanity that makes not only leadership, but the way we live, authentic, real, and most of all—human."

—Ralph Lauren

"Hortense le Gentil not only explains how our mindsets—often formed in childhood—can become mindtraps, she shows how to escape those traps to fulfill our true potential as leaders."

—Arianna Huffington, founder and CEO,
Thrive Global

"Hortense le Gentil's breakthrough book will enable you to unlock your humanity to reach your full potential. With the brilliant combination of deep psychological insights and personal stories, she shows how to discover the traps holding you back, find your authentic voice, and become an empowering and empathetic leader. This book is a must-read for every aspiring leader!"

—Bill George, author of *True North:
Emerging Leader Edition*; executive fellow,
Harvard Business School; former chair
and CEO, Medtronic

"In *The Unlocked Leader*, Hortense pinpoints the critical and genuine role leaders play—and the skills they must develop—in unleashing a true people-focused purpose and clear direction within an organization. She offers genuine practices that we, as leaders, can all employ to be the very best and most resilient version of ourselves."

—Corie Barry, CEO, Best Buy

"Hortense le Gentil provides both unique insight and inspiration for us to build more inclusive and emotionally informed collaborations and to lead based on genuine representations of our true selves."

—Tony Marx, president and CEO,
New York Public Library

"In The Unlocked Leader, Hortense le Gentil takes us on a beautiful and soul-filled journey to find the authentic leader within. Thank you for sharing this gift with all of us."

—Michelle Gass, president, Levi Strauss & Co.

"Hortense has done it again! Teaching leaders to lead with heart, empathy, and authenticity, her latest book is the ultimate guide to becoming the leader your team and company need. Full of powerful stories, years of on-the-job wisdom, and profound research, The Unlocked Leader is guaranteed to help you start leading more effectively today."

—Dr. Marshall Goldsmith,
New York Times bestselling author of The Earned Life,
Triggers, and What Got You Here Won't Get You There

"The Unlocked Leader is a gift for all on the journey to becoming authentic, human leaders. It illustrates our common challenges through real stories and offers actionable tools to develop our own leadership. A practical how-to guide to one of leadership's greatest challenges— knowing and being ourselves."

—Sarah Hirshland, CEO, US Olympic
and Paralympic Committee

"In The Unlocked Leader, Hortense le Gentil invites us on a magical journey, one that can truly free us from what has been holding us back and help each of us become the amazing, inspiring, human leader that we can be. The Unlocked Leader is the essential companion to every leader who aspires to lead with purpose and humanity."

—Hubert Joly, former Best Buy chairman
and CEO, author of The Heart of Business,
senior lecturer at Harvard Business School

"*The Unlocked Leader* is a masterful blend of psychology and storytelling that provokes us to bring to the surface the old beliefs and norms that hold us back as leaders and unlock the empathy and humility needed to be an effective leader in today's context."

—Ben Williams, CEO, Spencer Stuart

"This book holds the key to unlocking the best leader in all of us. Told with a charming fable, there are practical takeaways in every chapter. This book will not just make you a better leader, it will make you a better person."

—Chester Elton, bestselling author of *The Carrot Principle* and *Leading with Gratitude*

"*The Unlocked Leader* is an insightful, thoughtful book for anyone aspiring to become a better leader in all areas of their life. It clearly explains how both the conscious and unconscious mind can be developed to improve relationships, cultivate leadership, and just plain expand one's ability to interact with others on an elevated and comfortable level. I thoroughly enjoyed Hortense's easy to understand and comprehensive guide."

—Gail Miller, owner, Larry H. Miller Company

"By using stories we can all relate to and introducing the simple but powerful mindtrap, mindshift, mindbuild framework, Hortense does a masterful job of guiding the reader through a process of reflection, resetting, and rejuvenation with a broader focus and purpose. An easy read and powerful tool for managers at all levels."

—Chris Roberts, executive vice president, EcoLab Inc.

"*The Unlocked Leader* could not be better timed, as our new reality and multiple global challenges are forcing us to reassess who we are and how we show up in the world. Thankfully, Hortense has created a brilliant road map to enable us to emerge on the other side of this journey as more effective leaders: more in tune with our emotions, more empathetic, and more . . . unlocked."

—Cindy R. Kent, CEO, Everly Health

"This book is useful for leaders at every level, from the top of an organization to those leading from within a team."

—Pau Gasol, president, Gasol Foundation; member, IOC Athletes' Commission; former professional basketball player; investor and activist in projects related to sports and well-being

"*The Unlocked Leader* will quickly become an essential guide for every leader who is keen to move past what is holding us back. It is a beautifully written, inspiring pathway to becoming the most beautiful, biggest version of ourselves."

—Dr. Tasha Eurich, organizational psychologist, *New York Times* bestselling author of *Insight*

"*The Unlocked Leader* is the essential user guide for leaders looking to enhance their empathetic approach to leadership. With its three basic constructs—recognizing 'mindtraps,' planning for 'mindshifts,' and executing 'mindbuilds'—it's a practical playbook, filled with rich examples, reflections, and thought-provoking ideas. Highly recommended."

—Saugata Saha, president, S&P Global Commodity Insights

"What kind of leader do you want to be? Through personal stories and a simple process of unlocking our mental traps, *The Unlocked Leader* is a must-read for anyone aspiring to inspire and empower their teams to give the best of themselves. Behavior, courage, empathy, emotions, human connection . . . this book has it all. It will help you look deeper into your soul, conquer your fears, and be the best version of yourself. Hortense has a unique way to help people connect their heart and soul to their mind. This book will make you a better leader. It will make you a better person."

—Rafa Oliveira, international zone president, The Kraft Heinz Company

"An engaged workforce delivers results, or as Aristotle said, 'pleasure in the job puts perfection in the work.' Hortense shares how, when your empathy eats your ego instead of your ego eating your empathy, you create cultures where people want to work, deliver great results, and go home happy."

—Garry Ridge, The Culture Coach;
Chairman Emeritus, WD-40 Company

"Leaders must lead themselves first. In a world of exponential change, it's easy to fall into mindtraps. Hortense le Gentil gives us a brilliant book that teaches us how to tap into our human leadership and unlock our true superpowers for inspiring, leading, and creating value. Leaders, read this book today!"

—Sanyin Siang, Duke University Professor
and Thinkers50 #1 Coach & Mentor

THE
Unlocked Leader

HORTENSE LE GENTIL
WITH CAROLINE LAMBERT

THE
Unlocked Leader

DARE TO FREE YOUR OWN VOICE,
LEAD WITH EMPATHY,
AND SHINE YOUR LIGHT IN THE WORLD

FOREWORD BY JIM CITRIN, LEADER, CEO PRACTICE, SPENCER STUART

WILEY

Published by John Wiley & Sons, Inc., Hoboken, New Jersey.
Published simultaneously in Canada.

For general information on our other products and services or for technical support, please contact our Customer Care Department within the United States at (800) 762-2974, outside the United States at (317) 572-3993 or fax (317) 572-4002.

Wiley also publishes its books in a variety of electronic formats. Some content that appears in print may not be available in electronic formats. For more information about Wiley products, visit our web site at www.wiley.com.

Library of Congress Cataloging-in-Publication Data is Available:

ISBN: 9781394152933 (cloth)
ISBN: 9781394152964 (ePub)
ISBN: 9781394152971 (ePDF)

Cover Design & Illustration: Paul McCarthy

SKY10052954_080923

To Hubert

Contents

Part 2   Mindshift: Free Your Voice   65

Part 3   Mindbuild: Lead with Empathy   149

Foreword

For the past 35+ years, I've watched Hortense le Gentil flout conventional wisdom and take risks to stay true not only to herself and her values but also to her unflinching aspiration to help others reach their utmost potential. These are the very qualities that have made her a preeminent CEO and executive coach. So I read *The Unlocked Leader* knowing that it would be a powerful book for readers and leaders on a professional level. And it certainly achieves that objective. For me personally, reading this book has been profound, helping me make sense of a life-changing experience that has been both unbearably sad and magnificently uplifting. Hortense's approach of helping unlock the human leader in all of us by identifying and confronting mindtraps in order to move to mindshifts and finally to a mindbuild was just what the proverbial doctor ordered for me based on what unfolded in my life over the past 18 months.

She writes about the power of letting go, which, of course, sounds good in theory but makes any skeptical person wonder whether it actually works or will help you achieve your goals. And even if you do believe it could work, it is truly scary to release yourself from the beliefs you've grown up with that are core to who you are and that have led you to the success you've garnered up to this point in time. I experienced the power of *The Unlocked Leader* in the most real and sad way possible.

But I had no choice. And what I learned was to become the silver lining to a very dark cloud in my life.

For more than 25 years, I have been a partner at Spencer Stuart, one of the world's preeminent executive recruitment and leadership advisory firms, where I lead our CEO practice. I've had the privilege of helping clients with more than 800 CEO searches and successions, as well as board director and C-Suite appointments, for some of the world's best-known and most successful organizations. I've always taken pride in being fully responsive to clients, colleagues, and candidates, working long hours in a very hands-on way. This was based on the conviction that when clients retained our firm, with me as the team lead, I had to personally drive everything. Some of our competitors have senior partners bring in the business as rainmakers, only to pass off the project to more junior professionals to do the work. That was never the Spencer Stuart ethos; we take pride in doing the work.

This all changed when disaster struck. In late 2021, my beloved wife Lindsay became sick and was diagnosed with a devastating and rare form of cancer. We were living in London and she was on the world's most advanced clinical trial for her form of cancer. I continued to serve clients remotely while taking Lindsay to chemotherapy and immunotherapy sessions at University College London, to GI specialists at The London Clinic and the Cleveland Clinic London, and eventually to Royal Trinity Hospice.

It quickly became clear that I had no alternative but to let go. I literally could not do or drive every aspect of work as I had done for so many years. I also followed other aspects of Hortense's wise advice in this book: to be transparent, to be open and vulnerable, and, more than anything else, to be human. Often, I did Zoom meetings from the treatment locations, during which I always explained where I was and what was going on. What transpired were three unexpected things that I will never ever forget, that show the profound lessons of *The Unlocked Leader*.

First, not surprisingly, I was emotionally supported in my time of need. I was surrounded by love and trust by clients, colleagues, and candidates. Everyone understood what we were dealing with and going through and where I was doing my calls from. Work went from vocation to avocation, and it became a source of strength and joy that helped me cope and therefore be the best carer I could be for Lindsay. In April 2022, when Lindsay passed, the outpouring of love and support was beyond belief and the tribute that we established in her memory at London's Royal Trinity Hospice raised record sums of philanthropy. So I was being human, which helped me cope and therefore helped me care.

But two other things transpired that were a bit more surprising.

For one, my colleagues and partners stepped up. In a big way. Not only did our client service not suffer, but it was enhanced. As I stepped back it created the space for my colleagues to play more important leadership roles in our work. They got unparalleled experience with some of our most important assignments and in so doing accelerated their professional development, which led to enhanced satisfaction. I came to realize that my long-standing prior commitment to "own" the assignments I was leading was unintentionally blocking the opportunities for other partners and colleagues to shine. During the year of treatment, I openly told clients that I would do my very best to add value to the process, but that Alexis or Colin or Kate or Jason would be in the lead. Clients embraced this, as did all of my colleagues, who delivered and grew as top CEO search and succession experts and leadership advisors.

Third, as a consequence of this dynamic, and to my genuine shock, our CEO Practice had a record year, growing 55% from the prior year, which had also been a record. I experienced this on a personal and individual basis as well, achieving record commercial results.

How could all of this happen? By shifting my mindset and letting go of the mindtraps that had unknowingly held me back. By being real and true and honest. By not trying to do it all or be perfect. By creating the space for others to thrive. And today and moving into the future it offers a true gift. With my freed-up capacity, I now have a more open road to pursue my aspiration, which like Hortense's, is to help as many others as I can achieve their ultimate professional and personal satisfaction.

Going forward, I hope to continue to be the very embodiment of *The Unlocked Leader.*

Enjoy!

Jim Citrin, Leader,
Spencer Stuart's CEO Practice,
Bestselling author of *You're in Charge, Now What?,*
The Five Patterns of Extraordinary Careers,
The Dynamic Path, and Leading at a Distance

Acknowledgments

Hortense le Gentil

It has been a long journey. But we made it! And, I have so many individuals to thank.

I will start with my amazing agent, Jim Levine. Jim, working with you is a joy. Throughout the journey, you have always been present, positive, insightful, and kind. Thank you for your support, your generosity, and for being the embodiment of a human leader, someone who leads with empathy!

I will be forever grateful to Richard Narramore and the entire Wiley team, especially Jeanenne Ray, Jessica Filippo, Deb Schindlar, Susan Geraghty and our developmental editor, Kristi Bennett. I so appreciate how you immediately understood the value of *The Unlocked Leader* and committed to helping share its message with the world.

I have a special debt of gratitude to my coaching clients. I so appreciate your trust and the opportunity to learn from you. Working with you is a constant source of joy and a great honor.

My friend and advisor of many years, Maude Julien, has played a key role in supporting my growth over the years and has taught me so much about myself and about neurosciences. Maude is one of the world's foremost therapists, with a specialization in trauma and dealing with mental and behavioral manipulation, and her contribution to my understanding of mindtraps and mindshifts cannot be overestimated. She is also the author of *The Only Girl in the World*.

I wouldn't be where I am today without my mentor, Marshall Goldsmith, leadership coach, thinker, and author extraordinaire. Your example, unwavering support, and generosity over the years have encouraged and inspired me to get out of my comfort zone and grow as an executive coach and thought leader.

Special credits go to my "sister" Dr. Tasha Eurich, a brilliant organizational psychologist, and her husband, David, who helped shape the book in the early days of our journey; Jim Citrin, my friend of 35 years who somehow saw some kind of potential in me early on, has been a constant and incredible source of support, and generously wrote a beautiful foreword for this book; Gail Miller, whose story I share in the book, for being such a powerful source of inspiration for me; gratitude expert Chester Elton for introducing me to Jim Levine; and Krishna Patel, my Yogi master, whose wisdom has guided me over many years now.

My deep and sincere gratitude goes to those brave souls who took the time to review an early version of the manuscript and provided incredibly insightful and valuable feedback. They include leadership expert Bill George; Tony Marx, the extraordinary CEO of the New York Public Library; Penny Pilgram George, who has been a leader in the whole-person health and well-being space for more than two decades; and of course my husband, Hubert Joly, who I objectively believe exemplifies being "unlocked."

This book would not have been possible without my writing partner, Caroline Lambert, my soul sister. It has been an incredible adventure to write this book with you, Caroline. Your ability to understand my vision and help me organize, research, and translate my thoughts into beautifully written words and stories is pure genius. I am so indebted to you!

I am also deeply grateful to my personal support team, including Ysadora Clarin, Hasti Taghi, Olga Fedysiv, and Mitchell Winter. Thank you for keeping me organized and healthy, and for supporting me every day during this journey.

Finally, on a more personal level, my heart goes to my beloved and amazing children, Greg and Charlotte. Thank you for your love and constant encouragements—you've always been and will always remain my source of motivation; and to my parents, Marie-Françoise and Bernard, for your unconditional love.

Thank you to my in-laws, Denise and Jean-Louis, and to Stanislas, Johanna, Agathe, and Cyril for adding light in my life.

And last but not least, my profound gratitude goes to my beloved husband, Hubert. You are my grounding force. Thank you for your love, encouragement, support, patience, insightful comments, and immense sense of humor! Thank you for shining your light in my world. *What took you so long?*

Caroline Lambert

Working on this book has been an inspiration.

Thank you, Hortense, my soul sister, for this second book collaboration. Thank you for trusting me once again with your vision, ideas, and stories. Thank you for your energy, kindness, sense of humor, patience, friendship, and empathy throughout this crazy adventure. Working on this book with you has made me a better writing collaborator and helped me better understand and articulate why I do what I do.

Thank you, Jim Levine, for your unwavering support, guidance, and feedback. It has been an absolute joy and godsend to work with such a wonderful agent and human being.

These pages greatly benefited from the valuable input of several peer reviewers who were kind enough to read a first draft. A special thank-you to Hubert Joly, whose sharp eye and mind made this book immensely better.

I'm grateful to the Wiley team, and particularly Richard Narramore, Jeanenne Ray, Jessica Filippo, Debbie Schindlar, Susan Geraghty, and our editor, Kristy Bennett, for bringing this book into the world.

My heartfelt thanks to Ysadora Clarin for organizing countless Zoom meetings month after month.

Finally, my deepest gratitude and love go to my husband, David, and our daughter, Zoe, for their love, support, and understanding throughout late nights and weekends working on drafts and revisions. My world starts and ends with you.

"No one cares how much you know, until they know how much you care."

—Theodore Roosevelt

Introduction: The Fear of Being Human

Imagine an elegant office somewhere in the Upper East Side of New York City. One after the other, top business executives discreetly slip into the comfortable waiting room a few minutes before the door opens. They fear crossing paths with someone they might know. When that happens, both people awkwardly look the other way. This is the office of a renowned psychotherapist, and most of the business leaders who turn up there would rather keep their visits secret. Never mind that over one in five CEOs now seek therapy.[1] Even Richard Nixon's psychotherapist pointed out that leaders who seek help in times of stress are courageous and serve interests broader than their own.[2] Unfortunately, for many business leaders, openly asking for help and exploring their emotions is still too often perceived as a weakness.

For decades, the traditional view was that to be successful, business leaders had to be infallible, unflappable, in control, and fearless. These leaders appeared to be born leaders, naturally endowed with supreme intelligence, coming up with brilliant ideas and directives from the mountaintop that lower echelons were then expected to execute. They are what I call *superhero leaders*.

As an executive coach, I have worked with many such superhero leaders. These smart, goal-oriented, and successful executives are masters at leading with their heads. Yet there is something many of them are now realizing they should probably know but don't: how to lead with their hearts and souls, too.

This introduction was adapted with permission from "Leaders, Stop Trying to Be Heroes" by Hortense le Gentil, October 25, 2021, https://hbr .org/2021/10/leaders-stop-trying-to-be-heroes. Copyright 2021 by Harvard Business Publishing.

Hiding behind their superhero leader façade, they're not sure how they can connect differently with people at work. They don't know how to be vulnerable, authentic, and empathetic in a way that unleashes the best in others. In short, they don't know how to be *human leaders*.

This is a problem of global proportions—for these leaders themselves, but also for people around them, their companies, and by extension, for the world at large. Why? Because the multiple global challenges and crises we're facing have highlighted that superhero leaders are no longer what companies need.

This traditional approach to leadership is not what is most effective today because the world has changed, and so have employees' expectations.

A New Business Environment and New Expectations

The world, and therefore the business environment, has become increasingly more volatile, complex, and unpredictable. In 2019, for example, few people would have predicted that a new coronavirus was about to sweep through the world with devastating consequences. We're facing an unprecedented combination of complex socioeconomic, geopolitical, and climate challenges. To survive, companies must be increasingly fast and agile—and expect the unexpected. In the 1920s, a company listed in the S&P 500 could expect to live for 67 years on average; and today? Only 15 years. By some estimates, three-quarters of today's S&P 500 companies will be replaced by new firms within 10 years.[3] More than ever, companies must be environments of collaboration, flexibility, and innovation to survive and thrive. In today's business world, no one is infallible, and no single person, no matter how smart and experienced, has all the answers.

In addition to navigating a fast-changing and unpredictable environment, business leaders must also address new expectations and needs—starting with employees and, increasingly, shareholders. To give the best of themselves, employees want to feel respected, listened to, and inspired. They want to be seen, understood, and valued for who they are as individuals. Employees ponder over not only when, where, and how they want to work but also *why* they work.

Perhaps you think that these are soft, nice-to-have considerations rather than real business imperatives. But failing to pay attention carries a cost that may feel invisible but directly affects employees' loyalty and engagement, and therefore the company's bottom line. Employees rank respect from their leaders as the consideration that affects their engagement and commitment the most—ahead of recognition or appreciation, an inspiring vision, and opportunities for learning, growth, and development. Yet in March 2022, three in four employees felt that their company didn't care about their well-being.[4] Companies around the world suffer from an epidemic of disengagement.

In addition to being respected, seen, and valued, employees also seek leaders who feel human, not distant and perfect beings with whom they can't connect. There is clear evidence that members of a group consider as their leaders the individuals who put the collective interest before their own, work hard to make other people's good ideas happen, and are strongly perceived as "one of us" rather than someone striving to stand out from their peers. In other words, team members who are more concerned with getting things done than having their own way are the ones who emerge as genuine leaders. Why? Because they have more influence on the group than people who think of themselves as leaders and display the dominant behavior traditionally associated with it.[5]

In a context of changing expectations from employees and shareholders, as well as the demands of today's business environment, the traditional model of the seemingly unflappable, infallible, and fearless superhero leader doesn't feel like a great match. "We don't need another hero," Tina Turner was already singing in 1985. We need leaders who want to be a lot more like coach Ted Lasso of the Apple TV original series—the unassuming Midwestern football coach who transforms a struggling and fractious British Premier League club by bringing hope, joy, kindness, and an indomitable team spirit.

The most effective leadership today—at all levels, from the C-suite to small teams at the bottom of the corporate pyramid—isn't about technical expertise and having all the answers. In addition to articulating a compelling vision, it's about the ability to connect with people, understand their needs, and unleash their potential. As Mary Barra, the CEO of General Motors, put it, "At the end of the day, all businesses are about people first—because the only way we can build genuinely successful businesses is to build lasting relationships inside and outside the company," she told fresh graduates of the Stanford Graduate School of Business. "We do that by holding ourselves accountable, by doing what we say we are going to do, and by inspiring others to strive for something bigger than themselves."[6] Rita McGrath, a business professor at Columbia University, sees the evolution of business management in three eras: the first two were the eras of execution and expertise; today, she says, management has entered a new era of empathy.

Empathy is not often a word that comes to mind when thinking about business strategy and performance. It isn't often the first thing that comes to mind when thinking about successful business leaders, either. But a growing number of companies and business leaders are indeed realizing that the ability to put ourselves in someone else's shoes—whether a colleague, a customer, a supplier, a competitor, or a shareholder—and see the world the way they do has become a business imperative. Take Microsoft. In 2014, the company was losing ground. The tech giant, whose culture back then was known as brash and aggressive, had missed several fundamental technology shifts toward cloud and mobile computing. Then came a reboot. Over the following years, the company's fortunes turned, pushing the stock price up. Central to Microsoft's success has been a cultural revolution led by Microsoft's new CEO, Satya Nadella. What was that cultural revolution? Embracing empathy.

Empathy increasingly appears in job listings from mainstream employers such as strategy consulting firms, banks, or tech firms.[7] Understanding customers' needs, including the needs they might not articulate, is central to innovation and customer service. Microsoft's model-coach-care approach to management—model the behavior you'd like your reports to embrace, coach them, and care about them and what matters to them as individuals—relies on human connections, too. And the most effective teams are those made up of people of different backgrounds, experience, and perspectives who are able to understand, respect, and trust each other. Empathy is therefore critical at all echelons, starting at the top.

In short, to be most effective in today's environment, leaders must be *human leaders*.

Yet despite countless success stories and hard evidence advocating for leadership based on empathy, many leaders still cling to the good old superhero leadership approach.

So why do human leaders seem to remain the exception rather than the norm?

Because, as the saying goes, the longest journey we'll ever travel is the 18 inches between our head and our heart. Shifting from superhero leader to a more human approach is hard for several reasons. First, we are creatures of habit, relying on what we know. And many leaders have built their success on being goal focused. Over time, the specific brain network that focuses on setting and achieving goals has grown very robust. The tricky part is, when this specific network in our brain gets activated, the people-focused network—which helps you understand and connect with people's emotions—gets weaker. Effective leaders need to be strong in both, but few are.[8] So for leaders who for years have been so focused on goals, rebalancing their leadership approach takes effort and time. Because they've done well, why invest this time and effort? It's tempting and comfortable to keep doing the same thing.

Leadership coach Marshall Goldsmith, for example, might have chosen that path were it not for a conversation with a mentor, which, he says, changed his life. "You're too good at what you do," his mentor told him. "You're repeating the same day over and over again, and you're very successful. You will have a good life if you keep doing this. But you will never be the person you could be." Marshall realized that his mentor was right and learned a valuable lesson, which he's been sharing with the very successful leaders he coaches. "It's easy to think about the importance of unlocking your potential when things are going poorly," he says today. "But it's also good to think of this unlocking when things are going well and you're not under pressure. Because the temptation is 'I'll write this book *someday*, or I'll do this research *someday*,' but *someday* never gets here."[9]

There is a second reason why becoming a human leader is not easy. Seemingly fearless superhero leaders striving to become human leaders are facing one sizable obstacle, whether they realize it or not: their own fear.

The Sum of All Fears

When thinking about human leadership, many executives who spent their careers striving to be superhero leaders feel like the ground under their feet is no longer solid. "I was educated and trained to *never* show my feelings and vulnerability at work," one CEO recently told me. "Now you're telling me I have to? This is a real revolution."

Their fear typically manifests in three ways:

- **The fear of connecting with their own emotions.** For rational leaders used to flexing their analytical side, looking deep within themselves can feel intimidating, even dangerous. What are they going to find? Self-exploration might upset the applecart. Even more frightening, exposing their true selves might change how others see them. What if they appear weak? What if they lose control, authority, respect, and love?

  Frank,[10] the CEO of a very successful startup, reminded me of Forrest Gump, who in the movie of the same name kept running for no particular reason. Frank was working nonstop, juggling multiple projects and flying from meeting to meeting without taking a minute to reflect. At the same time, he struggled to properly communicate his ideas and to inspire his team, which left him frustrated and feeling alone. "Where are you running to?" I asked him. He didn't know. What he was running from soon became clear, however: he was afraid to look at his own emotions. A few months earlier, a close friend had died very suddenly. Frank was not only devastated, he also felt guilty—guilty that he was still alive, and guilty that he had not done more for his friend. So, he had to run, run, run to try to escape these difficult feelings.

- **The fear of chaos.** Many leaders believe that if everyone starts relating to their colleagues on a more personal level, it might unleash a tsunami of group hugs and kumbayas, which will detract from actual work. "Emotions do not belong in the office," one senior executive told me. How will they steer the ship if their role is no longer to fix all problems? What will happen when they let go of control? That thought leaves many of my clients feeling like trapeze artists without a safety net.

  During the worst of the COVID-19 pandemic, for instance, Bruce, a senior executive in a multinational company, was afraid that making space for emotions might open an uncontrollable floodgate of tears and grief. Where would it stop, he wondered, and what good would it do? Emotions would take over, bring everyone down, and undermine the work they all had to do. He also feared that if he stopped fixing problems himself, and instead focused on supporting people and bringing them together so they could find their own solutions, the business would unravel. Someone on his team aptly described him as a soccer coach who kept running on the pitch to play the ball.

- **The fear of failing.** Many leaders feel they don't know how to handle emotions at work—their own or others'. "What if someone on my team tells me they've just lost a parent or a spouse to COVID?," a client asked me. "Or if someone starts crying? I have no idea what to do or what to say!" Effectively leading with heart and soul takes skills and approaches leaders used to wielding their logic and analytical brain power may not have mastered yet. Even worse, these leaders who are used to success fear they could fail spectacularly. "I've been successful leading the old way," an executive told me. "I like the idea of becoming this new type of leader, but can I be as successful?" To many of us, the fear of failing is an old companion. Who has never felt a knot in the pit of their stomach before an important exam? Or when taking on new responsibilities at work?

Raise your hand if any of these fears—fear of connecting with our own emotions, fear of chaos, fear of failing—sound familiar!

Where do these fears come from? And how can we change in spite of them?

Although much is being said about *why* cultivating empathy and being a human leader is a good idea, very little is on offer when it comes to *how*. This leaves many leaders locked in their old approach.

How to Become a Human Leader

This dearth of "how-to" reminds me of a dream I had many years ago. I dreamed of my grandmother, who had died years earlier. "Go walk on the path of roses!" she told me.

The path of roses? I had no idea what she was talking about, but it sounded nice. My grandmother used to love roses, which she grew in her garden with great care and affection. From her perspective, a path of roses could only mean a sacred road to fulfillment, beauty, and happiness.

"Where is it?" I asked her in my dream.

"You already know where it is," she replied, smiling. "Now go!"

Then I woke up, furious and anxious.

Back then, I was feeling stuck. My life was filled with people who believed that to be successful, they were supposed to be superhero leaders. After years working in advertising and communications, I felt like I would have to fit into that leadership mold for my career to progress. That mold did not feel like me, but I feared I would fail if I veered from the successful and familiar path I was on, even though it was not working for me. Where was the exit? How could I find that "path of roses"? Although my dream suggested I already knew what to do and where to go, I didn't have the faintest idea.

Yet once I overcame my fear of change, I became an entrepreneur, leading teams of engineers in a sector I knew nothing about. There was no technical expertise I could contribute. So I was free to focus my energy on articulating an inspiring vision, as well as on motivating, supporting, and creating an environment in which everyone could deploy their unique talents, learn and grow, and become the best version of themselves. I finally felt at home.

Finding my own path to a different kind of leadership convinced me to help others find theirs.

So how can you become an effective human leader?

This is what this book is about. It offers a road map to your own path of roses. I have developed this road map based on my own journey, as well as my exploration of neuroscience, psychology, and spirituality, and years of coaching successful executives and entrepreneurs to become even more effective by leading differently.

Although this book focuses on leadership at work, each of us is a complete individual, not a sum of separate, isolated parts. As such, the process presented in this book applies to all areas of your life. The journey from superhero leader to human leader is one of deep inner transformation, because genuine and authentic empathy comes from within. It isn't about applying a few tricks and parroting the right words, which comes across as neither genuine nor authentic. To be able to profoundly understand and connect with others, we must first understand and connect with who we are and step into the fuller, truer version of ourselves. To do so, we must remove old beliefs and expectations that no longer serve us—what I call *mindtraps*. Part 1 will help you understand and identify these invisible *mindtraps* that hold you back from changing how you lead. Part 2 describes the process I use to help my clients create a *mindshift* to move past their mindtraps. Finally, Part 3 is about *mindbuild*—how you can build and anchor a new perspective and new practices that unlock the human leader within you. In this book, the journey from mindtrap to mindshift and mindbuild is presented in a sequential and linear fashion, to the extent possible. In reality, this journey typically isn't that perfectly sequential and linear— just like the earth isn't flat, even though it is often presented as a two-dimensional map.

Throughout these pages, you'll find many companions traveling by your side. Some are main characters whose stories run like threads across chapters. Others play supporting roles, appearing only to illustrate specific points. Also keeping you company is an imaginary child who's looking for his path of roses; his fable opens each chapter. Besides (hopefully) making this book enjoyable, these stories are meant to deepen your transformation. Although facts and research will speak to the analytical and linear circuits in your brain—often known as your "left" brain—these stories are meant to activate your more intuitive, emotional "right" brain. I also hope that you will recognize part of yourself in these stories and that they'll encourage, inspire, and support you throughout your journey toward human leadership.

My purpose with this book is for you to know what took me years to realize: that my grandmother was right. The key to unlocking that fuller, truer version of ourselves lies within us, and this book is to help you find it, so you can lead with empathy and shine your light in the world.

PART 1

Mindtrap: Identify Your Lock

To become human leaders, we must be able to lead not only with our heads but also with our hearts and souls. Cultivating empathy starts with ourselves: to connect to and understand other people's perspectives and emotions, we must first connect to and understand our own. Over time, we have formed beliefs and perspectives that shape our view of ourselves, others, and the world. Our journey toward becoming a human leader requires identifying which among these beliefs and perspectives have become obstacles to leading with empathy—our mindtraps. Part 1 is about understanding how mindtraps are born (Chapter 1), how to identify our own (Chapter 2), and uncover what—and who—hides behind them (Chapter 3).

CHAPTER 1

When the Keys to Past Success Get in Your Way

How Mindsets Become Mindtraps

Once upon a time, there was a child who lived by the sea. He spent time sitting on a rock, drawing circles in the sand with a stick. Each day, the tide would cover the circles, and each day, the child would draw the same circles.

"Hello, my friend!" the child hears one day.

The child looks around, but no one else is there.

"Down here!" the voice says.

The child sees an oyster clinging to a rock.

"Are you an oyster like me?" the oyster asks.

"Can't you see I'm a human?"

"You don't feel like a human," the oyster says. "All humans are gifted beyond measure. They can move mountains and travel the sea. They can dream and make the impossible possible. Do you ever dream of what lies beyond these shores?"

The child has never thought about it.

"Then your gift is locked inside your shell, just like my pearl."

Humans can make the impossible possible? The thought makes the child's heart sing. "How do I unlock my human gift?" the child asks the oyster.

"I don't know," the oyster says. "I'm not human."

They are both silent for a moment. A fisherman walks by. Here is a human who's traveled to other shores, the child thinks. Perhaps he can help.

"Do you know how I can unlock my human gift?" the child asks the fisherman after greeting him.

16

"Look for the path of roses," the fisherman says.

The child has heard of that path of roses. People in the village talk about it sometimes. "How do I find it?"

"That's for you to figure out," the fisherman says. "But you won't find it if you stay here."

Although the idea of leaving his village scares him a little, the child decides to go look for the path of roses and unlock his human gift. So he says his goodbyes and walks away from his village with a heart full of hope but also trepidation about the journey ahead.

Before reaching the forest, the child comes across a horse in a meadow. The horse is walking around in a circle, sniffing the grass, which is dry and patchy. The horse's ribs are showing through its dull coat, which is taut as a drum.

"Are you okay?" the child asks.

"I'm hungry," says the horse. "I don't know what's happened to my grass. It used to be green and thick, and I was happy here. But now it's all dried up, and I cannot find enough to eat."

Looking a bit further out, the child sees a green meadow. "Why don't you move to that meadow over there?"

For the first time, the horse looks up. "I had not seen that meadow before! The grass indeed looks thick and green over there," the horse says. "But I cannot go."

"Why not?" the child asks.

"Because of the electric fence!" the horse says. "It will hurt me if I try to go over there."

"What fence?" the child asks, perplexed. "I don't see any fence."

"I grew up in this meadow and I know it's here," the horse says. "The farmer put it up when I was little to keep the cows out, so they wouldn't walk to my meadow and eat all my grass. That's how I was able to grow big and strong. But every time I walked too close to the edge, it gave me a big jolt. I can still feel it, so I'm not going anywhere."

How strange, the child thinks. The horse is locked inside an invisible prison. As he walks away, the child then wonders: Is he, too, trapped within invisible fences?

* * *

How do the beliefs and outlook that get shaped in our brain over time become obstacles that stand in our way? In other words, how do mindsets turn into mindtraps? And why is it so difficult to see them in ourselves? This chapter will explain the following:

- How mindtraps get created
- How we can tell that a mindtrap is standing in our way
- Why we don't see ourselves as clearly as we think

The Birth of a Mindtrap

From an early age, Harry, the CEO of a Fortune 500 company, strove to be perfect. At school, teachers saw mistakes as weaknesses to be eradicated rather than opportunities to learn. At home, Harry's mother expected him to excel in everything he did, pushing him to fulfill the limitless potential she saw in him. Harry concluded that striving for perfect grades and number-one rankings would lead to elite universities. Elite universities would in turn pave the way to prestigious employers, where a perfect performance would be the ticket to a high-flying career. In short, striving for perfection was the road to success.

This perfectionist mindset served Harry well. It motivated him to excel, and excel he did. By age 30, he'd made partner at a top strategy consulting firm. From his perspective, everything was going swimmingly. Then he went through a 360 assessment. Although he scored very well on many dimensions, his team's engagement ranked lower than the firm's average. Harry was shocked. How could that be? He didn't know what to do with that feedback, so he ignored it. A few years later, after he'd become a senior executive in another company, another assessment again revealed that his team was not as motivated as the rest of the company. Again, Harry met the feedback with disbelief. The company was doing significantly better than a few years earlier, which suggested he was doing everything right. And if the problem was not with him, then it had to be with his team.

Harry hadn't yet realized that his relentless pursuit of perfection in himself and others meant that he often viewed others as obstacles, rather than partners. His mindset and behavior hampered human relationships and, by extension, effective teamwork and collaboration. A belief that had served him so well had become a limitation on his path to become a better leader. His mindset had become a mindtrap.

Many of the beliefs, mindsets, or perspectives that our brains concoct are meant to serve us well. In fact, this is precisely why they take shape in the first place. Initially, these beliefs earn us approval, love, admiration, or acceptance. Who doesn't want all that? These instinctive pulls are almost impossible to resist, particularly at a young age, and they influence our behavior and our choices. Children instinctively strive for their parents' love and protection because it is vital for their survival and proper physical, psychological, and emotional development.

As we grow up, we typically want to feel that we belong to a group of like-minded friends or allies, who provide protection, collaboration, and understanding. Many teenagers desperately want to conform to whichever "tribe" they choose. In high school, my client Tanisha, a senior executive, badly felt the need to belong and make friends with popular girls and have fun. Yet earning that acceptance and becoming part of that group was incompatible with being a good student, which wasn't considered cool. But Tanisha wanted and needed to excel at school. To square that circle, she learned to show only part of herself: to her teachers and parents, she was the smart and successful student; and to her friends, she carefully hid her good grades and drive to learn so she could be the cool, friendly, and funny girl who, like them, felt that school was "lame," and good students, hopeless nerds. Only when she graduated top of her class did her friends discover that she'd been one of these "nerds" all along.

This instinctive need to belong extends far beyond family, friends, and colleagues. Our often-unconscious quest to fit in results in our absorbing collective beliefs and world views, such as social, cultural, national, or religious norms. Like the air we breathe, these norms are all around us, and they rule many aspects of our lives, from gender or family roles to work behavior. Whether we want it or not, they shape us by influencing our view of how we are supposed to behave or what it means to be a good friend, neighbor, parent, colleague, or leader.

Star athletes like Olympic swimmer Michael Phelps and NBA player Kevin Love, for example, have said how social values about men in general, and male athletes in particular, have influenced their behavior. "For the longest time, I thought asking for help was a sign of weakness because that's kind of what society teaches us," Phelps says. "That's especially true from an athlete's perspective. If we ask for help, then we're not this big macho athlete that people can look up to."[1] Love echoed the same sentiment. "Growing up, you figure out really quickly how a boy is supposed to act." he said. "You learn what it takes to 'be a man.'

It's like a playbook: *Be strong. Don't talk about your feelings. Get through it on your own.* So for 29 years of my life, I followed that playbook."[2] These collective norms determine how many leaders view their role and how they should behave. They also influence how we define success or failure, or even happiness.

So, on the one hand, these mindsets we adopt are useful. They bring us love, recognition, a sense of belonging or the drive to succeed, among many other things. On the other hand, they can also bind us. The problem arises when our mind behaves like the horse in the fable at the beginning of this chapter. We, too, can get stuck, bound by invisible fences of our own making that prevent us from moving forward. This is when a mindset becomes a mindtrap.

Why does it happen? How can something that initially helps us become an obstacle? Whether suddenly or slowly, in big or small ways, everything and everyone changes—ourselves, others, and our environment. We become older; we change jobs; a new colleague joins our team; a pandemic spreads across the world; someone becomes sick or dies; children are born, grow up, and make their own lives. Yet the mental constructions that live largely in our unconscious do not always adjust. We keep thinking and behaving in the same way, or we cannot let go of old emotions. This is how mindsets that have outlived their purpose become mindtraps. What once served you no longer does. "I'm good at this" or "This is how I've always done it" turns into "It no longer works."

Patrick, a senior executive in the insurance industry, was a math whiz who had built a successful career on his technical expertise, which propelled him from promotion to promotion. He spent his free time solving math problems and approached most challenges as equations to be solved. He was now being considered to head one of the group's subsidiaries, which involved interacting with the board of directors and the media. The CEO of the group was hesitating, however, wondering whether Patrick had the emotional intelligence that the new position required. Although he was impeccably charming and polite, he was also distant, keeping all interactions with his colleagues and his team strictly about work and carefully avoiding any whiff of conversation that might veer toward the personal. He managed his team as a group of variables to be organized in the right order to play their part and saw no need to communicate any sense of direction or purpose. In short, the technical competence that had underpinned his success and gave him a sense of pride and identity was no longer enough. Why? Because to succeed in his prospective role, emotional intelligence was far more important than technical skills.

As top executive coach Marshall Goldsmith puts it: *what got you here won't get you there*. In fact, he has listed what he calls the "20 bad habits of leaders"—behaviors that often contributed to their success but are getting in the way of their becoming better leaders. These include traits like the need to show people how smart we are, not listening, blaming everyone but ourselves, the need to win at all costs and in all situations, or exalting our faults as virtues.[3] Together with Sally Helgesen, he's also identified 12 habits that more often stand in women's way, such as a reluctance to claim one's own achievements and overvaluing expertise.[4]

Cul de Sac

How can we tell when a mindset has become a mindtrap? There are many symptoms. Sometimes we clearly feel locked or stuck in our own lives. We realize we've reached a dead-end and that something must change, but we don't always know how to move forward. When the COVID-19 pandemic broke out, Andrew, the CEO of an industrial company, understood that what he'd always thought was good leadership was no longer appropriate. The situation was unprecedented, and for the first time, he didn't know what to do. He could see that the company's employees were under a lot of strain, worrying about their jobs, their loved ones, and the future in general, and struggling with lockdowns. How was he supposed to fix this? How could he help his teams? He knew that he could no longer behave the way he had so far—speaking more than he listened, coming up with solutions to fix all problems, and telling people what to do—because for the first time, he didn't know what to say and what to do. But he also had no idea what the alternative was. Like Andrew, we sometimes clearly see that we're stuck. Perhaps we feel our career is not progressing the way we'd like, for example, or our relationships feel stale. Have you ever felt you've hit a wall, but you're not sure why or how to move forward?

Bill George, the former CEO of Medtronic, remembers the moment he realized a mindset had become a mindtrap. From the time he was nine years old, his father told him he wanted Bill to become a CEO of a large company and be the leader he'd never been. This drove a young Bill to run—and lose—seven times for student council in high school and college. When he was around people who he felt were important, he would try hard to impress them. While working at Honeywell, he was one of two candidates to become the next CEO. He changed the way he behaved, careful to say the right thing at the right time. He also changed the way he dressed, wearing cufflinks, which he didn't typically wear, at board meetings just to impress board members. Then one day, driving in his car, he looked into the rearview mirror, and what he saw was a deeply unhappy man. He had contorted himself so much to fit who he thought he had to be to fulfill his ambition that he had lost touch with who he truly was. His mindset had become a mindtrap standing in his way. He had received several offers to become the CEO of Medtronic, a company whose purpose and culture he felt aligned with. But he'd turned them all down because he felt the company was too small. Once he realized he was trapped in a mindset that no longer served him, Bill decided to accept the Medtronic offer, and immediately he felt that he'd come home.

In many instances, however, we are not aware that a mind-trap is keeping us back. For example, the same situation keeps happening again and again, but we put the blame on someone else's shoulders. Remember perfectionist Harry, the CEO of the Fortune 500 company, and his teams' engagement feedback. Or we fail to see that our body acts as the canary in the coal mine, signaling a mindtrap at work. At a time when my first marriage broke down but I felt I could not leave, for instance, I became severely ill. Yet it took me a while to see the connection. Similarly, every time one of my clients faced a difficult decision, he suffered some sort of accident and injured himself.

Mindtraps may also crop up as arrogance or, alternatively, as imposter syndrome. Can you think of people who come across as full of themselves? People who rarely miss an opportunity to remind everyone that they've graduated from a top university, for example. People who never ask for anyone's opinion and, whenever it is offered anyway, won't listen. When encountering setbacks or delays, they are quick to become frustrated with their team and to blame others. Yet, this façade often hides deep insecurity and can easily crumble.

My client Blake, however, suffered from imposter syndrome. When I met him, he was a successful entrepreneur who'd left his corporate job several years earlier to start a company that offered bespoke workspace solutions. He was full of innovative ideas but struggled to convince his business partner. For the first few years, their partnership had worked well. Then came a time to innovate and for the business to take more risks. Because his partner didn't share the same vision for the business and didn't want to take risks, Blake's ideas never went forward, which confused staff members and produced mediocre results, all of which left Blake frustrated and unhappy. Yet he systematically deferred to his partner's opinion.

Blake was convinced that becoming a successful leader required graduating from a top university, being hyper-analytical, and showing no emotion. This was the direct and indirect message he'd absorbed from a young age. Throughout his childhood, his father had hammered into him how important academic results and prestigious degrees were. Unaware of how much his family's opinion had influenced him, he then noticed only the evidence that supported that view. Famous business leaders who were his role models fit that profile. So did many of his former colleagues. Unsurprisingly, by the time I met him, he was convinced that this was not an opinion, but an absolute truth. The problem was that Blake was none of these things: he'd been a mediocre student, and his strengths were vision, creativity, and human relationships, rather than analytics. Because he didn't fit the profile of a stereotypical leader, Blake feared he would never succeed by himself. So he'd partnered with a hyper-analytical, much older and confident graduate from a prestigious university who fit his idea of a successful leader, but was no longer the partner he needed. Unaware of the mindtrap that sabotaged his self-confidence, he couldn't see that he stood in his own way.

Other common symptoms of mindtraps include burnout, unhappiness, or even depression. This is what Tanisha, the senior executive who as a teenager hid that she was a good student to make friends with the cool crowd, experienced later in life. She kept showing only the part of herself that she thought others wanted to see. Regardless of the time of day, she always wore makeup, and her hair was impeccably styled. She perfectly fit in at work, always behaving as was expected, never making waves. There was one sizable problem, however: by the time I met Tanisha, she was profoundly unhappy at work. Her boss did not respect her. She was also unable to express values that were important to her. After George Floyd died at the hand of the police in Minneapolis, she wanted to organize conversations at work. But when her boss told her this was out of the question, Tanisha relented because she felt she might lose her job if she insisted. Yet she was angry and dispirited. She no longer wanted to hide part of who she was, but she didn't know how to show her whole self without blowing up her entire life.

I've experienced these mindtrap symptoms several times—
and still do sometimes! After the company I co-created in the
metal recycling industry made headway on the technical front,
we had to secure regulatory approvals to develop the business
further. For months, I spent enormous energy lobbying countless people from industry and government bodies. This wasn't
what I enjoyed doing, but it had to be done. Worse, I made little
progress. And the more resistance I met, the harder I pushed.
Until one evening, I met a friend for dinner, and he pointed out
how worn out I looked and sounded. "Why do you keep banging
your head against the wall?" he asked, after I explained what I'd
been doing. "You need to find a way around it!" Then, I broke
down. Until that conversation, I hadn't seen that this was exactly
what I'd been doing. Just like during my teenage years, when
I trained as a competitive show jumper, I kept getting back on the
horse every time I fell. The way I was raised, persistence and commitment were essential qualities. But without realizing, I had
equated exploring any other path with giving up and failure,
which felt unacceptable to me. Once my friend helped me see
that mindtrap, I was able to change tack. Instead of pushing for
approvals that might take a long time to come, if they came at
all, we instead partnered with clients who were already certified,
which removed the need to get the approvals altogether.

So whether we know we're stuck but can't see what stands in
our way, or we don't even see that we're stuck at all, why are we
often so blind to our own mindtraps?

For one overarching reason: we don't know ourselves as
much as we think we do.

How Well Do You Know Yourself?

Do you know yourself? If or when someone asks you this
question, what do you say? Most of us are highly confident we
do. We know what we like and don't like. We're confident we

know how we'd react to specific situations. We feel we have a good grasp of our major strengths and weaknesses—both personality traits and skills.

The problem is, we don't see ourselves as well as we think we do. In fact, organizational psychologist Tasha Eurich points out that, although 95% of people she surveyed said they were either somewhat or very self-aware, we often are deluded.[5] In reality, we all have blind spots about who we really are and how others see us. One of my clients, for example, firmly believed she was terrible at math, even though she'd graduated from a top university known for its demanding math curriculum. Conversely, have you ever had a colleague or a boss who was convinced that they were excellent at their jobs, even though they weren't as good as they thought? My guess is you have.

Why don't we see ourselves as clearly as we think? For three main reasons: self-awareness is not always comfortable, we're blind to our unconscious, and change is not easy.

First, seeing ourselves clearly is not always pleasant or comfortable. Most of us have no problem admitting to our strengths, but it is less comfortable admitting what we could do better, especially in areas that we value. Even if we've been told about growth mindsets and learning from failure, many of us still consider these areas of potential growth as baked-in weaknesses or shortcomings, particularly if they don't fit our own ideals and values. For example, if like Harry, the perfectionist CEO, you've been conditioned to think that you should be perfect, it isn't easy to take on board any signal suggesting that you're not. It feels much more comfortable to ignore these signals or dismiss them as "it's not me, it's them." There is often a gap between how others perceive us and how we perceive ourselves: our brains make snap judgments and take useful, but often misleading, shortcuts. Yet we do the same with our own selves, too. It is therefore tempting to dismiss other people's perceptions about us as an error, even when they happen to see us more clearly than we do see ourselves.

Second, we're blind to our unconscious, and we grossly over-estimate how much we control our own selves. Our minds are like icebergs, a small fraction of which is visible while the rest remains hidden under water. Many of our beliefs and perspectives, particularly those that we've held for a long time, have become so automatic and part of who we are that, like the submerged part of the iceberg, we don't see them. This means that most of our mindtraps live in our unconscious, away from the glaring spotlight of our own awareness. Not only are we unaware of their control over us and our actions, often we've also forgotten how they even formed in the first place. Take Bill George's story. Although he'd pushed his father away, he'd subliminally adopted his message that success meant being CEO of a large company. It took him years, and becoming utterly miserable, to become aware of it.

Do you remember what happened when you were a baby? I don't, either. Yet the way our brain develops during the first seven years of our life greatly influences the way we socialize, interact, and communicate with others later in life, including our ability to empathize.[6] During these early years, millions of neural connections are created, based in part on how our parents and caregivers respond to us. These connections create the foundation of our brain architecture.[7] But there are so many, and they formed so early in our lives, that it is difficult to trace why or how they took shape.

There is a third main reason we're blind to our mindtraps. Becoming aware of what keeps us back is the first step toward change, and change is not easy. First, we get used to behaving a certain way, and the more neural pathways get activated, the stronger they become. This makes old habits hard to change. When my client Bruce became a senior executive in a multinational corporation, for example, he realized he could and should no longer decide everything for everyone. His micromanagement demotivated his teams, and he genuinely wanted to step into a role that created space for others to flourish and grow.

Through conscious effort, he managed to change his attitude and behavior. Then a crisis hit: the company's supply chains were disrupted, which created significant production and distribution challenges. Without realizing it, he returned to his previous top-down management style. In a time of uncertainty and anxiety, his trusted old habits automatically reemerged and took over.

Also, our unconscious survival instinct can make change difficult. Unless the status quo becomes untenable and threatening, it feels safe. Change, however, carries potential but also means uncertainty, and uncertainty means risk. This explains why fear and anxiety often crop up in the face of change. So even if our mindtraps become obstacles, we can unconsciously find comfort in keeping things as they are.

* * *

Our mindtraps, whatever they may be, are mindsets and beliefs that once served us well. As such, let's take a second to thank them. Yet they're now like guests who outlast their welcome, and they need to go. In this chapter we've identified how to recognize common symptoms of mindtraps, and why we've perhaps not seen that they'd become obstacles. But wait, if we don't know what our exact mindtraps are, how can we remove them to unlock ourselves and move forward? We first need to identify them and understand who has been hiding behind them.

SELF-REFLECTION

1. **The birth of a mindtrap**
   - What mindset do you feel has helped you most so far? Is it still helpful?
   - Is there an area in your life in which you feel you're repeatedly confronting the same situation?

(Continued)

2. Cul de sac

- Can you identify a situation when you either didn't know how to move forward or spent enormous energy taking action but made little or no progress?
- Do you sometimes feel you're playing a part instead of being your genuine self? When and why?

3. How well do you know yourself?

- Have the results of a 360 assessment or any other type of feedback ever surprised you? How?
- Can you identify your main strengths and areas that you need to improve?

CHAPTER 2

Uncover Your Inner Obstacles

Which Mindtrap Is Holding You Back?

After meeting the horse trapped in his meadow by invisible fences, the child keeps walking through the forest, wondering where to find the path of roses. How can a small child who's never left home know the way? Impossible! the child thinks. It starts raining. Tired, he slumps on a tree stump. An old woman approaches.

"Are you waiting for someone?" she asks.

"I'm waiting for a princess on a horse," says the child.

The old woman thinks for a few seconds. "There aren't many of those around here," she says. "Why don't you wait inside my hut? You're getting all wet."

The child agrees and follows her. Soon they reach the hut and step into a warm room. An old man sits by the crackling fire.

"Why are you waiting for a princess on a horse?" the old woman asks as she throws another log into the hearth.

"I am looking for the path of roses, and I cannot find it by myself."

The old man looks up. "Why not?"

What a strange question, the child thinks. "I'm too small and too young, and I've never traveled far from my village. Also, I have a poor sense of direction. So I need someone to show me the way."

The old man looks at the child more closely. "You are not so small, and you seem very clever to me," he answers. "After all, you've found us!"

The child doesn't buy it. "But everybody knows that only princesses on horses know the way!"

* * *

Hiding behind the fears described in the introduction—
the fear of connecting with our own emotions, the fear
of chaos, and the fear of failing—mindtraps come in all
shapes and forms. Because they are born out of our unique his-
tories and perspectives, they are as specific to us as our finger-
prints. But even though the details are exquisitely unique, these
traps often fall within three main patterns or a combination of
these patterns:

- Trauma
- Identity
- Role

This chapter reviews what each pattern looks like. Then it
examines how they influence the way we communicate with
others—a key element of human leadership—distorting how we
position ourselves.

The Long Shadow of Trauma

Andrew, a top executive in a large industrial group, was in the
running for his company's CEO position at a relatively young
age. His chances looked excellent: he had climbed at record speed
through the company's ranks thanks to his good performance,
and he was the departing CEO's first choice. He was a bit surprised to be considered for the job, being much younger than
other candidates. At the same time, he'd so far seemed confident
in his own abilities. Then the decision was announced: to everyone's surprise, the board had chosen another, older candidate as
the company's next CEO.

What had happened? Andrew was aware that his meeting
with the board had not gone as well as it could, and he asked
the executive search company in charge of the process for
feedback. He was told that, during the meeting, he'd seemed like

a completely different person from the calm and confident executive they knew. He'd spoken fast and incessantly, leaving little or no space for board members to interject and even interrupting whenever they could ask follow-up questions. He kept veering off on tangents that were irrelevant to what the board members wanted to know. Andrew was perplexed, unsure what this was all about. When he asked what he could do to avoid making the same mistake in the future, the recruitment partner advised him to seek coaching.

Andrew came to see me, eager to find out what explained his behavior and open to anything. When we discussed the board meeting during a coaching session, it seemed clear to me that a mindtrap was involved. Could he describe what he'd been feeling during the board meeting? Andrew thought for a moment. He'd felt very anxious, like an imposter who didn't deserve to be considered for the CEO role. Had he found himself in this kind of situation before, I asked, or did it remind him of anything? At first, Andrew drew a total blank. But as we kept probing together, an incident he had entirely forgotten suddenly flashed through his mind. He remembered his final oral exam as a business school student.

Andrew had been a brilliant student, although he was younger than most of his peers. He'd received good grades throughout the program and felt confident that his final oral exam, which largely determined whether he'd graduate or not, would go well, too. As he stepped into the exam room to make his oral presentation, there was therefore just enough adrenaline running through his veins for him to feel properly focused, and the panel of three professors, the audience of fellow students, and what was at stake didn't overly intimidate him. During his presentation, however, one of the panelists kept stepping in and asking provocative questions instead of waiting for question time. Before Andrew had a chance to respond in full and properly defend his views, the professor would interrupt him, distorting what he'd just said. Andrew was shocked, as he'd not expected to be grilled so aggressively, particularly while he was still presenting. Within a few minutes, his confidence had completely evaporated, and he was unsure what to say or do. Panic took hold of him, and he froze, unable to think clearly any longer. "Young man, your emotions and your nerves are written all over your face," the panelist concluded in front of the audience. "I can promise you one thing: you'll never become CEO." Andrew was devastated.

What Is a Trauma?

When Andrew and I first discussed the incident, he didn't realize that he'd suffered a psychological trauma, which then ossified into a mindtrap. But wait. Isn't trauma the result of a horrific experience? Not necessarily. Psychological trauma is what happens when an event or a series of events trigger in you strong and difficult emotions like intense fear, shame, pain, powerlessness, or grief that destroy your sense of safety and overwhelm your nervous system. Seen in this light, an incident that can externally appear as relatively benign can result in psychological trauma, and a situation that can be traumatic for one person might not be for another. Trauma becomes a mindtrap when these initial emotions and the overwhelming fear they unleash are not properly processed. Our brain is unable to shelve traumas the way it does other memories, so they keep casting a long shadow over how we think and behave long after the event or the series of events that triggered the trauma is over.

Imagine our brain as a house with distinct rooms. Regular memories are like pieces of furniture that get placed in the proper room: the sofa goes into the living room, the dishwasher in the kitchen, and so on. Now imagine that your car, instead of being parked in the garage, ends up in your living room. So every time you step in to watch TV or sit with your friends, here is your car getting in the way, utterly out of place and impossible to ignore. A traumatic memory is like that car. Until you're able to park it in its proper place, it will at best narrow your perspective, and at worst, make your life difficult.

The post-traumatic stress that many combat soldiers and assault victims experience is an acute illustration of this mechanism: any sound, smell, visual, words or situation that evokes the initial trauma triggers overwhelming stress and involuntary survival reactions, even when they're no longer facing a real threat.[1] Imagine an unhealed, festering wound. How would you react if you thought something or someone might press on it? Andrew's oral exam was like that wound. Even though he had graduated and even forgotten what had happened, the trauma stayed alive in his unconscious, influencing his beliefs and behavior. Even though he was unaware of it, his high-stakes presentation in front of all board members, who would determine whether he'd get the CEO job or not, reminded him of his oral exam. Afraid that the same situation would happen again, he'd preempted any possibility that someone could destabilize him by dominating the conversation and making sure no one else could speak.

I experienced something similar after a thief broke my car window to steal my purse on the passenger seat while I was on the way home from work one night. The shock of the violent intrusion had left me frozen, and cars behind me started honking, adding to my panic and helplessness. Panic morphed into terror as I realized the thief could now find my keys and my address inside my purse, and my two young children were home with their nanny. When I made it home, everyone was fine. I blocked my credit cards, changed my locks, and had my car window repaired. I put it all behind me—or so I thought. For months, I was inexplicably thrown into a sudden panic every time I walked under a streetlamp, or a movement occurred in my peripheral vision when I was driving. It wasn't until I sought treatment from a psychotherapist that I understood what was going on. Although I was convinced I hadn't seen the attacker, my senses had actually registered him approaching from the side, crossing the halo of a streetlamp, and my brain remembered it as a trauma. So every time I found myself near a streetlamp at night, my brain kept reliving the incident and the terror that came with it. Once I received eye movement desensitization and reprocessing therapy, a technique that helps heal from trauma by rewiring the brain, I was able to properly process the memory of the attack by moving it to its proper neurological place—like the car in the garage. Once the memory had been properly parked, I no longer relived it.

Inherited Trauma

So our own traumas, big and small, can turn into mindtraps. But our mindtraps are sometimes associated with somebody else's trauma. Whether the impact of trauma can or cannot be biologically transmitted across generations through our genes is still hotly debated among scientists. Yet even if our genes are not involved, our parents, teachers and social, national, or religious environment can undoubtedly influence our views and beliefs—including when it comes to trauma. For example, David, a senior executive in the financial industry, had developed a technical expertise that was highly valued at work, but he was always suspicious and hypervigilant. He suspected colleagues wanted him to stumble and often wondered when mistakes happened whether some of his team was out to sabotage him, which resulted in aggressive outbursts and conflicts. Constantly on the defensive, he was careful never to let his guard down and share anything personal or ask his team members about their aspirations and hopes. He was therefore unable to genuinely connect with people at work and struggled to advance his ideas, but he blamed others for his lack of traction.

"You sound like you're fighting a war!" I remarked during one of our conversations. "Whose war are you fighting?" He looked at me as if a door had suddenly opened in his mind. Although David was born and had grown up long after World War II, his parents and grandparents had had to flee and hide from the Nazis, always on the lookout for possible danger and afraid they might be betrayed. Growing up, David had absorbed his parents' and grandparents' mindset that the world was a dangerous place, and that no one outside the close family circle could be trusted. The very outlook that had kept his family alive during the war, however, became a significant obstacle at work, undermining David's relationships with colleagues and his impact. Identifying this inherited mindtrap and bringing it to David's consciousness was the first step toward shifting his perspective.

In addition to psychological trauma—whether big or small, our own or others'—the second common mindtrap pattern has to do with identity, or how we see, define, and value ourselves.

How Do You Define Your Identity?

When psychologist, researcher, and teacher Shawn Achor launched a survey on happiness and human potential among Harvard students, his friends were puzzled. Of course Harvard's high-achieving students were going to be successful! What could they possibly be unhappy about? Yet, some four in five Harvard undergraduate students reported experiencing depression at some point over the previous year—far more than the national average.[2] So Achor surveyed some 1,600 students to figure out what set apart the one undergraduate in five who was still happy.

He found that the problem starts when students who've typically been in the top 1% of their class from preschool to high school, made the honor rolls, and blew the SAT out of the park walk into Harvard on their first day. These serial overachievers suddenly realize that, for the first time in their lives, they could be part of the 50% of students that are below average. As Shawn Achor jokingly put it to them, 99% of Harvard students do not graduate in the top 1%. None of them found it funny.

This realization sends students down one of two paths. A minority of undergrads recalibrate their view of themselves to find what they're best at. They learn to manage stress and spend time with friends and doing things they find fulfilling. These students typically end up performing much better both at school and after they graduate. Yet this group makes up a very small minority. Most students instead get trapped in a downward spiral. Focusing on their weaknesses, they drop extracurricular activities, no longer spend time with friends, become increasingly stressed, and believe the admissions department made a mistake choosing them. They burn out and get lower grades.

The second group suffers from an identity mindtrap. Much of how they view and value themselves is bound with being at the top of the academic heap. There is nothing inherently wrong with that, but when this mental construction is challenged and doesn't adjust to different circumstances, these students become undone. They're hardly alone. Many of us suffer from an identity mindtrap at one point or another in our lives. Just ask non-working parents what happens to them when they become empty nesters.

This loss of identity struck me much earlier in life, when I decided to give up competitive show jumping in my late teens. For years, I had invested an enormous amount of time, effort, and focus into horse riding. Only a few years after I stepped back did it become clear that, without realizing, I had also invested a significant part of my identity. First, I left my native France and followed my dream to experience life in the United States, where I studied for a while. When I came back home, however, my American degree was not valued as I'd hoped it would be, and I struggled to figure out what to do next. I became disoriented. I was home, but no longer in a world where I'd been known and valued for my riding talent and experience. Who was I, if no longer a successful showjumper? It took me a while to revise how I defined and valued myself, and to find a way forward.

This is a mindtrap many successful professionals, particularly men, experience when they retire without much preparation: they suddenly lose the social status and power their job once gave them, and from which they drew much of their identity.[3] This is exactly the kind of mindtrap that afflicted Ray, a CEO in his late 60s. When he first came to see me, he was furious—and scared. He'd just been told he would have to retire. But Ray didn't want to retire, and he felt angry being pushed out. He still had a lot to contribute, and he felt retirement was signaling not only to him but also to the rest of the world that he'd reached the end of his useful life. He was also scared: having focused on his career for so long, he had no idea who he was without it. He worried that, without the status and stimulation his job gave him, he would become invisible, as endless and empty days would send him spiraling prematurely into old age.

When one single area of our lives—whether career, children, cause, or vocation—absorbs an overwhelming share of our time, energy, and attention, it can easily hijack our entire identity. Without a good dose of self-awareness or planning our next chapter in life, we risk becoming undone like the Harvard undergraduates in the happiness study. At the height of a career that left her with no time and space for anything or anyone else, movie star Cameron Diaz, for example, was acutely aware of this mindtrap. "I just went 'I can't really say who I am to myself,' which is a hard thing to face up to," she later explained to fellow actress Gwyneth Paltrow. "I felt the need to make myself whole."[4] So in 2014, she decided to quietly step away from acting. During a hiatus that ended up lasting eight years, she invested in health and biotech startups, wrote a book, launched her own organic wine brand, and also got married and had a child.

NBA champion Pau Gasol, however, was forced to prepare for his life after basketball when a navicular stress fracture on his left foot pushed him off the basketball court. Although he was determined not to let his injury dictate the end of his basketball career, he wasn't sure he would be able to play again. So he used his rehab not only to get back into shape but also to prepare for his transition out of pro athlete life. After two years, Gasol was able to come back to the basketball court and play in the Tokyo Olympics—after which he was ready to retire on his own terms.[5] Olympic gold medalist Michael Phelps summed it up when he said, "I always thought of myself as a swimmer and that's it. Now I try to think of myself more as a human. And that's a good way to live."[6]

The identity mindtrap works both ways, however: we tend to overly tie our self-worth to what we've accomplished and what we're good at, but we sometimes limit ourselves where we feel we're not. Wendy, the CEO of a nonprofit, had trouble with her organization's board. She was unable to present and defend her views, particularly on financial matters. So, the board made decisions when she should have, which she ended up resenting. During our coaching sessions, we uncovered that she believed finance to be an area for which she had no aptitude and never would. Where did that mindtrap come from? She grew up in a family who lived for mathematics. Her parents were math teachers, and her brothers all became engineers. She didn't share their penchant, however, which made her feel deficient and isolated. In her mind, this gradually crystallized into "I'm bad at math," even though she'd studied advanced mathematics in high school and graduated successfully. She carefully sidestepped anything having to do with numbers, which led her to the nonprofit field but also further fed her mindtrap. By the time I met her, she was systematically deferring to the board, feeling both inadequate and resentful. Her identity mindtrap had led her to repeat at work the dynamics she'd experienced as a child. She needed a mindshift to reset her relationship with the board and step fully into her CEO role.

All the "I'm not good/strong/competent/brave etc. enough" or "I'm far too . . ." are mindtraps following this common pattern. They hold you back if you believe they are innate traits that cannot change and should be hidden. So do identities built on labels, titles, or on how you compare to others: "I'm a CEO" or

"I'm an athlete" or "I'm an engineer" or "I'm the smartest in the room." The trap is to invest your self-value in these identities, so you find it hard to let them go. But what happens when you're no longer CEO or your new job no longer requires that technical expertise? Or when you don't have clear answers to a problem? Or you come across someone smarter or stronger than you? You become afraid to change how you lead, unsure of who you are. So, spend some time reflecting on how you see yourself, and what you value about yourself or would like to change.

What of the third common pattern of mindtraps? In addition to trauma and identity, roles can become obstacles we need to shift to become unlocked.

Are You Wearing the Right "Suit"?

Frank, the CEO of a very successful scale-up was "running" non-stop to avoid confronting what he felt after the sudden death of a close friend. In addition to grief, he also felt guilt—guilt that he had not done more for his friend. By being hyperactive, he was desperately trying to push aside the feeling that he was unworthy and had done something wrong. His behavior affected his relationship with his team and the company's performance though: he never stopped long enough to share his vision properly or ask about how his colleagues were doing, so the flurry of activities and demands left his team confused, discouraged, and burned out. So did his mounting frustration about their performance, which he found disappointing. His life outside of the office suffered, too: he had no time for his partner and for his friends.

Frank's mindtrap was largely about roles—or what psychologist Carl Jung labeled archetypes. He had a precise idea of what kind of person and actions made a good friend, and deep down, he believed that he'd fallen short of his own standards, a view he then refused to confront. Whether we realize it or not, we all carry norms about the many roles that we fulfill in our lives. What does it mean to you to be a man, a woman, or perhaps neither? A good parent, child, sibling, friend, or neighbor? What do you think makes a good colleague? And a good leader? We draw answers to these questions from people around us, but also social norms. For example, NBA player Kevin Love believed for a long time that men, particularly pro athletes, had to be tough and should not share their feelings. This mental picture did not include looking after one's mental health, he believed. I remember how my grandmother firmly believed that women shouldn't work, and my mother that being a veterinarian wasn't a "woman's job."

Imagine a jacket or suit that is the wrong size or cut for you. Unless you decide to go for clothes that fit you, you have a problem. Either you manage to squeeze yourself in and feel very uncomfortable, or you can't even wear them at all, and you start feeling that you, instead of the clothes, are the wrong size and fit. This is what this type of mindtrap is like, closing on us in two ways. Either we conform to a role that does not, or can no longer, fit us, which often results in anger, depression, or burnout, or the gap between who we are and who we think we should be cannot be bridged, which can leave us feeling guilty, ashamed, inadequate, or fearful. For Kevin Love, conforming to his model of how a male athlete should behave, which meant ignoring and hiding his depression, eventually culminated in a debilitating panic attack during a game, for example. And Frank felt a crippling guilt because of the gap between his mental picture of a close friendship and how he thought he'd failed to spend enough time or help his friend before he died. Whether we play a part that no longer fits us or are unable to bridge the gap between who we are and who we think we should be, we cannot move forward, endlessly trapped in either being or trying to be someone we're not or struggling to accept who we are.

This type of mindtrap is pervasive in business environments. According to research from the Deloitte University Leadership Center for Inclusion, 61% of employees feel they have to hide part of who they are at work. This sentiment is particularly prevalent among members of the LGBTQ community and African Americans, with about 8 in 10 people feeling this way. Yet even 45% of straight white men also report hiding part of who they are.[7]

This is a problem for many professionals in leadership positions, regardless of their background. For decades, the superhero leader model dominated the collective business psyche, sending legions of business graduates and corporate professionals on a quest to become, or pretend to be, an impossible ideal. This has left scores of executives feeling either like imposters for projecting a façade that doesn't reflect who they truly are or inadequate for failing to tick the "right" boxes. For example, Andrew, the executive who had a traumatic exam experience discussed previously in this chapter, had internalized the professor's view that a CEO shouldn't show any emotion and had to project unshakable confidence. Besides being stuck in a trauma that torpedoed his interview with the board, he had for years carefully been hiding any doubt or insecurity behind a mask of false confidence.

However, entrepreneur Blake, who'd started a company offering workspace solutions, could not hide that he hadn't graduated from a prestigious university or wasn't highly analytical—attributes that he believed any successful business leader should have. He couldn't pretend to be that kind of leader. Because of this unbridgeable gap, he struggled to embrace who he was and instead viewed his strengths as weaknesses. Unable to fully trust his own ideas, he therefore doubted he could ever be successful on his own. This mindtrap led him not only to find a business partner who fit the stereotype of the superhero leader but also to let that partner decide the direction of the business.

Steve Jobs, the cofounder of Apple, could easily have fallen into a role mindtrap. His adoptive parents, who hadn't studied beyond high school, had promised his birth mother that he would get a college degree. After six months in college, however, he felt he was wasting his time. But instead of ignoring his conviction and staying in college, he embraced his own idea of what success and being a good son could look like by dropping out to stop spending his adoptive parents' scarce financial resources on tuition, and starting his own business instead.

Trauma, identity, role. These three types of mindtraps undermine our potential and become obstacles to being an effective human leader. Why? Because mindtraps greatly affect how we relate not only to our own self, as we've seen, but also to others, which is at the heart of human leadership.

The Consequence of Mindtraps

Mindtraps affect how we communicate with and relate to other people—and therefore how we lead. Throughout our daily life, we automatically—and often unconsciously—step into different "parts," depending on whom we interact with. We effortlessly move from behaving like a parent or a child, for example, or a colleague, manager, or teammate when we step into the office. We each have a repertoire of multiple personas—slightly different aspects of the single person we are—and we navigate from one to the other, depending on the situation. But we are sometimes miscast, and this is when the problem arises. The "parent" in you, for instance, can sometimes come up when guiding a junior colleague or leading a team, and you may step in instead of letting them find their own solutions.

For example, Blake, the entrepreneur previously mentioned, stepped into the wrong "part" when interacting with his business partner, due to his mindtrap. This created an imbalance. Instead of approaching the relationship as one of equals, he systematically deferred to his partner's opinion and judgment, even though their respective visions of the business were very different. Because he didn't trust his own ideas, he also struggled to communicate them clearly. So he had trouble motivating and mobilizing his team, which left him frustrated. Too busy battling his own insecurities, he was also unable to inspire a sense of safety and optimism in those around him. During our conversations, he realized that he'd positioned himself as a "child" with his older business partner, which influenced his behavior not only with him but also with everyone else in the company.

So did Wendy, the CEO of the nonprofit who believed she was no good with numbers. When she talked to me about board meetings, she became agitated and nervous. Her breathing changed, and she automatically justified decisions that were not being questioned. Once she became aware of it, she realized that she had been stepping into the part of the "little girl" with board members and had to reposition herself as the CEO.

What about David, who had inherited his parents' war trauma? Because he was trapped in seeing everything and everyone as a threat, he used his own specialized knowledge as a defensive weapon. At work, he behaved like a "lecturer," droning on about arcane technicalities to show off his unique expertise while also jealously guarding his turf by making sure nobody could quite understand and become a rival. At the same time, he misread everyone's intentions as malign and cast himself as a "victim," which was the source of constant conflicts.

* * *

To be able to shift our mindtraps out of the way, we must first uncover and identify them. Your mindtrap is related to a trauma, to the way you define your identity, or to some idea of the role you're in that no longer fits you. It could involve a combination of all these "families" of mindtraps. In any case, your mindtrap affects how you relate to other people, locking you into behaviors that weaken your leadership. Having identified the mindtrap(s) that prevent you from stepping into a truer, bigger, and more empathetic version of yourself, we must now uncover their roots—the voice that has planted and fed the perspective that no longer serves you.

SELF-REFLECTION

1. The long shadow of trauma

- Revisit a difficult moment of your life, the first that comes to your mind. How did you feel in that moment? Do you still feel the same when thinking about it? If so, chances are that your mind is trapped in a trauma.
- Do you find yourself overreacting in specific situations? Do these situations remind you of other circumstances?

2. How do you define your identity?

- What do you value most about yourself or do you feel the proudest of? How would you see yourself if this disappeared?
- How much self-worth do you link to your accomplishments, rather than to who you really are?

3. Are you wearing the right "suit"?

- What is your definition of being a successful leader? A good colleague, parent, child, or friend? What does it mean to you to be a man? Or a woman? Or do you stay away from gender identity? Whom do you consider to be role models for each definition?

4. The consequence of mindtraps

- Do you often have the same conflict with the same person?
- Do you find that you sometimes struggle to make yourself heard?
- Think of the main relationships in your life. Do you feel you've positioned yourself in the right way?

CHAPTER 3

Find the Source of Your Mindtrap

Whose Voice Is It?

When the child tells him why he thinks he cannot find the path of roses, the old man sitting by the fire is dumbfounded. Only princesses on horses know the way to the path of roses? Who has ever heard of such a thing? "This sounds like nonsense," he tells the child. "Who said that?"

The child has never been asked that question before. Everybody knows this to be true! So after thinking hard, the child explains he's read about it in books and newspapers, and he's heard it many times and from many people—his parents, his neighbors, his friends.

The old man cups his ear with his hand. "Who?"

The child repeats what he's just said. The old man shakes his head, a quizzical look on his face and his hand still cupping his ear.

"He only hears what he wants to," says the old woman to the child.

"It's a gift," the old man explains. "That way, I don't get confused and lose my way, because the only voice I hear clearly is my own."

* * *

All of us have absorbed and carry within us external voices that have shaped how we view ourselves, other people, and the world. These voices often live in our unconscious, working in the background like the operating system of a computer, influencing our behavior. Although their influence is often positive, they can also feed and perpetuate mindtraps. Once we have identified the mindtrap we want to shift, the next step is to identify and isolate the voice associated with it.

There are two main types of voices that influence us:

- The voices of specific individuals, especially if they wield authority over us, such as parents, teachers, and siblings
- Collective "voices," such as religious, cultural, or social norms

Some voices support us, and others feed our mindtraps. Which voice or voices do you listen to? The good news is, we can choose.

Only by first identifying the voice behind our mindtrap can we then separate it from our own to operate a mindshift.

The Voice of Authority

"I feel like I'm chained to a stationary bike," Claire told me when I first met her. "I'm pedaling as hard as I can, but I'm going nowhere." To me, she felt like a walking contradiction. On the one hand, she reminded me of a field mouse, diminutive and taking little space. She looked uncomfortable with her own self, trying to hide behind enormous eyeglasses. At the same time, she was like a pinball of energy. She constantly pushed herself, working long hours, swimming to exhaustion, while striving to be the perfect leader, colleague, mother, friend, and wife. At home, she kept everything tidy and impeccable—she sheepishly admitted that she even cleaned before her housekeeper arrived! Why was she pushing herself so hard but felt she wasn't good enough? And what was the mouse-versus-pinball duality all about?

Although it was immediately obvious to me that she was exceptionally bright, full of ideas, and very perceptive, Claire was struggling to find her place within her new company, which made it difficult for her to operate at her full potential. She'd been hired to fill a senior position that had just been created, which involved shaking up the status quo. Her colleagues, who didn't always fully understand or value what she was trying to do, didn't appreciate having to change their old habits. Her ideas didn't get much traction, and she did not feel trusted or even appreciated. To top it off, her father, whom she admired and adored, had died of cancer a few years earlier, and she was still feeling equally angry and disoriented.

We explored her history to identify the source of her mind-trap. As a child, she'd loved to draw and daydream. A lateral and visual thinker, she'd naturally relied on her sharp intuition and emotional intelligence to guide her. But her mother kept getting irritated that Claire's mind, as she put it, was as disorganized and messy as her bedroom always was. "Stop being so weird," she used to tell her. "Are you insane? Why can't you be normal like everyone else?" At the same time, Claire had grown up admiring her father, a famous and very successful businessman who never seemed to rest. Linear, rational, and always busy, he seemed to have little interest or time for emotions, and his vision of success was very straightforward: "Get results!"

As we worked together, she realized that, to gain her parents' approval, she'd worked hard to become more like her dad. She traded art for finance and intuitive daydreams for double-entry accounting. Following her father's example, she was not only pushing herself without respite to always get more and better results that always left her unsatisfied, but also setting aside the emotional part of herself. In addition, she was trapped in her mother's belief that the more creative and intuitive part of herself was crazy and messy, and therefore had to be repressed and silenced. The problem was, she was spending an enormous amount of energy to be someone she was not, and she'd lost sight of her own identity. Then when her father was diagnosed with cancer but refused to undergo treatment, she felt abandoned and angry. Why hadn't he been willing to fight for her?

Until she accepted, valued, and gave herself permission to voice her whole self—not only the smart, analytical, and hard-charging Claire, but also her caring, creative, and intuitive side—she would never feel that anyone else accepted and valued her. Without realizing, she'd let her mother's voice and her father's vision of life live on in her mind and dictate her choices and behavior.

Our parents have an enormous influence on us during the first years of our lives, so we often carry their voices. Even though former CEO of Medtronic Bill George, for example, wasn't close to his father, he realized well into his career that he'd been following his father's idea of professional success. He'd worked hard to become CEO of a large corporation—a path that had left him feeling miserable. Also, when Doug Conant, the former CEO of Campbell, lost a job much earlier in his career and started working with a coach, he realized that he'd behaved very much like his parents and teachers expected him to, rather than let his true nature shine through. And what about Fortune 500 CEO Harry, introduced in Chapter 1, who struggled to understand why his team was disengaged and to accept that it had to do with him? He carried his mother's voice, which fed an ambition and perfectionism that undermined his potential to become an outstanding human leader, until he was able to let it go.

Other authority figures such as teachers, coaches, or religious leaders often shape our minds and our lives through words and actions that, when they no longer serve us, can lead to mindtraps. And more recently, social media platforms, while opening a space where people can find more diverse views and voices, have also created a new type of authority figure: social media influencers, who shape not only fashion and advertising but also perspectives and behaviors.

Once top executive Andrew remembered how he'd been told during an oral exam that he would never become a CEO, he realized that the voice of the professor who'd berated him had been profoundly shaping his perspective on leadership and his behavior for many years. First, that voice was directly related to his disappointing board interview when he was being considered for the CEO position. How so? His unconscious still feared not only that his unfortunate exam experience could happen again but also that his professor's prediction would come true, and he wouldn't become CEO. So he overcorrected by speaking too much, which ironically meant he ended up with the very outcome he was trying to prevent: he didn't get the job. Aside from the trauma of his exam experience, he'd taken onboard the professor's view that CEOs should never let their emotions show. They had to be in control, unflappable in the face of unforeseen circumstances, and always have answers and solutions to the toughest questions and problems. The professor's perspective had become a commandment, rather than an opinion. But did Andrew agree? How did *he* think a leader should be?

Someone else's voice is not only what they say but also their actions and example. This is the kind of voice that Ray, the CEO in his late 60s who was reluctantly pushed into retirement, kept hearing. Why was he so afraid of retiring? He'd invested much of his identity into his position and the social standing it gave him, and he wasn't sure who he was without it. Yet, even as we worked together to rebuild his sense of self and to prepare the next chapter of his life, his fear persisted. Something else kept feeding his mindtrap. So I asked him: When he was thinking of someone having retired, what came to his mind?

Ray described a disheveled old man wearing pajamas and slippers, who barely saw anyone and spent most of his day at home sitting in his armchair, watching TV. This was clearly what he feared he would become. Yet I had trouble reconciling the man in front of me—friendly, caring, funny, sharp, and elegant with his crisp white shirts—with the picture he was describing. "Does it remind you of anyone?" I asked him. Suddenly, the penny dropped. When he was a boy, he'd spent some years living with an uncle, who'd raised him like a son. Much older than his parents, his uncle retired while Ray still lived with him. In Ray's eyes, he'd suddenly aged well beyond his years and started living a small and empty life, seemingly forgotten and waiting for death. His uncle had become someone he couldn't recognize. Ray had unconsciously absorbed his uncle's example as a cautionary tale of what would happen once he stopped working. In short, he kept hearing his uncle's "voice"—or in this case, seeing his image, which he'd interpreted as destiny rather than choice.

Senior executive Mateo also developed a mindtrap rooted in a parent's example. When I met him, Mateo was a workaholic who never celebrated his achievements, which he systematically downplayed and considered insufficient. Feeling he should never be satisfied or rest on his laurels, he thought his team could always do better, too, which left them feeling pressured and unwilling to take risks. Where did Mateo's mindtrap of never doing enough come from? Whose voice was pulling the strings of that mindtrap?

When we explored these questions together, Mateo realized it was related to his father's story. Mateo grew up in a happy home, with loving parents who were well liked and respected within the community and who enjoyed hosting friends. He was raised striving to do more and better, thinking he could achieve anything if he worked hard. This happy life crumbled when his father became a drug addict and lost his job, however. Friends stopped visiting, and money became tight. Joy and laughter evaporated. Ashamed of his father's demise, Mateo tried everything he could think of to help him recover. Thanks to his drive and hard work, Mateo was able to support his mother and siblings. But he couldn't save his father, which fed a deep sense of guilt and failure. Mateo kept thinking that if he'd done more or taken a different approach, his father would have gotten better. Decades after his father's death, he was still feeling guilty and inadequate, unable to shake the conviction that he was never doing enough. Although the drive to always do more, which was directly related to his father's demise, had initially helped him support his mother and siblings, it had become a mindtrap that weakened his leadership.

We can also develop mindtraps imitating the actions of people we admire. This is what happened to one of my friends, for example. He'd learned a lot from one of his mentors, who had many qualities and was very funny. But that mentor's sense of humor was often at other people's expense. My friend thought he should be funny, too, and started behaving like him, making fun of others—until someone else he admired too suggested that this was neither who he was, nor who he wanted to be. "You need to be your own person," my friend was told, "not some imitation of him. That's not the way you usually treat people."

Our mindtraps can therefore spring from the words or actions of a person in a position of authority or influence. But the voices we carry with us can also be like echoes, reflecting the collective influence of religious, cultural, or social norms.

The Power of the Collective

After 26 very successful years at the investment bank, Mark, a managing director and partner at Goldman Sachs, was debating whether to throw his hat in the ring to become the next CEO of a nonprofit focused on nature conservation, a cause close to his heart. After Mark reviewed the pros and cons at length with his coach, it seemed clear that the job was perfect for him. Yet he was hesitating to even apply. When his coach asked him why, he said, "If I get the job, I'm afraid of what my Goldman partners will think."[1]

We are essentially social animals. For prehistoric humans, survival largely depended on joining forces with others. Every group functions according to a set of rules and norms. Because of both our instinctive drive to belong and how our brains affect each other, our views and behavior can be shaped by a community— whether our immediate circle of family and friends, colleagues, or a wider group, such as a country or an entire culture. Have your friends and family, with your best interest at heart, ever offered unsolicited strong advice or opinions that influenced yours? Or like Mark, have you ever contemplated a choice and found yourself worrying about what other people might think? These are all collective "voices" at work, and like individual voices, they sometimes feed our mindtraps.

In the TV show *The Good Doctor*, Dr. Asher Wolke, who grew up in an Orthodox Jewish community, has cut all ties with his family and rejected faith altogether, choosing to study science to become a doctor. Dr Wolke is gay, which is not acceptable to his ultra-religious family, particularly to his father, a rabbi. More broadly, who he is isn't compatible with his community's religious precepts. This is a situation familiar to many members of the LGBTQ+ community who grew up in families and communities espousing traditional beliefs and values that view homosexuality at best as a sin, or at worst an abomination. This is a powerful collective voice, which in many cases forces on individuals who don't fit its rules a difficult choice: either hide and negate who they are or be shunned. Besides being powerful, that collective voice is also enduring. The acute dissonance between individual identity and the internalized collective voice often results in multiple mindtraps such as guilt, depression, and low self-esteem or self-loathing.[2]

More generally, cultural and social norms create collective voices that can give rise to mindtraps when they're at odds with who we are or undermine our sense of belonging. To belong to a group, we must understand the explicit but also the silent codes of the multiple environments that we navigate, and we must adjust accordingly. The question is, are we able to adjust and still be ourselves, or do we end up bending ourselves out of shape? When I was 15 years old, I left my parents' rural home to attend a posh high school in Paris. When I arrived, the culture shock couldn't have been more brutal. I was an athletic tomboy who'd been attending the local co-ed school and spending my free time riding horses. I found myself in an all-girls school with students wearing heels, pantyhose, pearl necklaces, and sporting long manicured nails. On weekends, I was expected to attend social get-togethers organized for the offspring of "good" families, where we played cards or, later, danced, instead of spending my time in stables and at show jumping competitions. I felt like an alien with my flat Mary Janes and white socks, thrown on a planet whose social and dress codes I didn't understand.

It took me a year to learn these codes and carve my own niche. I was never going to become part of the pearl necklace brigade, who had no interest in studying, because they were expected to marry well and stay home raising children rather than aspire to a career. But I ditched the little girl appearance, wore boots and black trousers, and started rebelling against the strict confines of our traditional school—enough to become visible and earn the respect of other students, while keeping my grades up. I was no longer a pariah, but I hadn't forgotten who I was, either. Understanding and playing with the social codes became like a game for me.

Seeking acceptance while developing and maintaining one's own identity is particularly challenging when straddling two very different cultural or social worlds. This is a struggle that many children of immigrants face, stretched between the world and culture their parents came from and the norms that prevail in the country where they live. Straddling different social norms can be just as difficult. In *The Hate U Give*, a novel by Angie Thomas turned into a movie of the same name, Starr Carter is a teenager who lives in Garden Heights, a predominantly African American inner-city neighborhood where gangs rule. But she attends Williamson Prep, a private school in an affluent and predominantly white neighborhood where everyone is college bound. "Garden Heights is one world, Williamson is another," says Starr, "and I got to keep it separate." When she's at school, she becomes another version of herself—one that doesn't use slang, even when her white friends do, and is approachable. "Basically, Williamson Starr doesn't give anyone a reason to call her 'ghetto,'" she says, "and I hate myself for doing it." At the same time, she struggles to fit in her own neighborhood, where she hardly knows anyone her age—and teenagers she does know often tell her she thinks she's too good for Garden Heights.

Tanisha, the top executive who hid her good grades from her friends so they wouldn't think she was "uncool," also illustrates a slightly different but similar version of the tension that collective voices create. When I met her, she was still hiding part of herself and her identity behind perfect makeup and perfect hair to project what she thought was required to be accepted in her work environment. But the root of her mindtrap could be traced all the way back to her school days.

We all feel the pressure to conform. But how far are you willing to go? Professional basketball player Kevin Love believed that sharing to anyone about himself and his feelings, let alone asking for any kind of psychological help, was a weakness that could derail his career and make him seem weird. Whose voice was behind that mindtrap? He cannot single out anyone in particular. "These values about men and toughness are so *ordinary* that they're everywhere . . . and invisible at the same time, surrounding us like air or water," he says. But this is a voice from which he had to distance himself when his mental health deteriorated.[3] This collective voice is at work in every "people say that . . ." or "women/men/children are not supposed to . . ." or "leaders should . . ." Whenever I ask my clients, "Who said that?" they are unable to tell me, because these voices indeed surround us like air or water.

The safety that being part of a group provides therefore comes at a price: its collective voice can drown individuality. Writer Joseph Campbell often told the story of a newborn tiger left among goats after his starving mother died while pouncing on the flock. The flock adopts the baby tiger, who grows up believing that he too is a goat. He grows up meek and skinny, eating grass and bleating, unaware of the strength of his jaws or of his roar. One day, an adult tiger comes across the flock of goats, which scatters at the sight of danger. The adult tiger is stunned to see a young member of his species eating grass and bleating. "What's wrong with you?" he asks. "You're a tiger!" The young tiger just bleats that he's a goat. The older tiger takes him to his den. He tells the youngster to take a bite from the half-eaten gazelle he's kept from the previous day. "But I only eat grass!" says the young tiger. Unable to convince him with his words, the older tiger shoves a piece of meat down his throat. The youngster gags a little at first, but as he swallows the meat, a newfound strength runs through his body, and he lets out a small roar. And with that, he realizes what his true nature is.[4]

Are you a tiger pretending to be a goat? Are you comfortable with the collective voices of your family, community, and work environments, or are you forgetting who you are? When we listen to voices that keep us from expressing our true nature and fulfilling our own needs, we risk becoming like the hungry ghosts of Buddhism, the creatures with thin necks and big bellies who are never satisfied regardless of how much they eat.

Which Voice Do You Listen To?

A Native American legend tells the story of an elder who teaches his grandson. "There are two wolves waging a war within me," he tells the young boy. "One is evil, anger, hate, and despair. The other is good—he's kindness, love, and hope." He explains that the same war takes place in the heart of every person.

The boy thinks for a moment. "Which one will win?" he asks.

The grandfather smiles. "The one you feed."

We all have the power to choose which voices we listen to. On April 14, 1865, a mere six weeks after his second inauguration, President Abraham Lincoln and his wife, Mary, went to the theater in Washington, DC. The 56-year-old president had accomplished a lot during his first term. The devastating Civil War had ended a few days earlier when Confederate General Robert E. Lee surrendered to Union General Ulysses S. Grant at Appomattox, and the Union would survive. In 1863, Lincoln had issued the Emancipation Proclamation, which legally ended slavery in the southern states. Just a few days before going to the theater, he'd made a speech from the portico of the White House detailing his plans for the country, which included introducing limited Black suffrage. The speech most likely set actor and Confederate supporter John Wilkes Booth into motion. Shortly after 10 pm, Booth fired a single shot inside the Ford theater, fatally wounding Lincoln, who was in a box watching the show.

After Lincoln died the next morning, several items were found in the pockets of his black coat and given to his eldest son. Together with a cufflink, a monogrammed handkerchief, a pocketknife, and several pairs of spectacles was a brown leather wallet, which contained several press clippings. In addition to documenting major events that helped the Union win the war, several articles praised Lincoln, his performance as president, and rejoiced at his re-election. For all his accomplishments, the President often suffered from severe depression, and had his entire adult life. The clippings were the voices he chose to hear whenever his spirits were low.[5]

One positive voice can be enough to keep negative ones at bay. When she was 13 years old and living in Greece, entrepreneur and author Arianna Huffington came across a picture of Cambridge University in England. She was so taken that she decided that she had to be a student there. When she told her friends and her father, they all told her it was a ridiculous idea. First, she was a girl, and this was the 1960s. In any case, surely it was too expensive. Not to mention she lived in Greece and had no connections. How could she ever make it to one of the most prestigious universities in the world? No way.

Had she let that collective clamor worm its way into her mind, her life would have been very different. But Arianna was determined, and so was her mother, who decided to investigate whether there was any way for her daughter to make her dream come true. A few years later, at age 16, Arianna moved to England to attend Cambridge on a scholarship, where she later became the first woman president of the university's famous debating club, the Cambridge Society, before becoming a successful entrepreneur and writer. Her mother's unwavering support played a critical role in her success. "I don't think that anything I've done in my life would have been possible without my mother," she told writer Sir Ken Robinson, a specialist in education and creativity. "My mother gave me that safe place, that sense that she would be there no matter what happened, whether I succeeded or failed. She gave me what I am hoping to be able to give my daughters, which is a sense that I could aim for the stars combined with the knowledge that if I didn't reach them, she wouldn't love me any less."[6] She decided to listen to her mother's voice. Even more importantly, she listened to the inner voice of her own passion, which gave her what she needed to ignore the nay-sayers.

What about Mark, the investment banker and committed environmentalist who hesitated interviewing for a job at a conservation nonprofit? When his coach heard he was worried about what his colleagues at Goldman Sachs would think if he got the job, he stopped right in his tracks and looked Mark squarely in the eyes. "Dammit, Mark," he exclaimed. "When are you going to start living your own life?" This outburst convinced Mark to listen to his own voice. He interviewed for the job and became the next CEO of the conservation nonprofit, a role he fulfilled with great success and that gave him a deep sense of purpose and joy.[7]

* * *

Once you've identified the individual or collective voices that have been feeding your mindtrap, then what? What do you do with this discordant cacophony? It's time to create some distance and make space for your own voice to emerge and be more clearly heard.

As Yoda says to Luke Skywalker in *The Empire Strikes Back*, "You must unlearn what you have learned." This is what the mindshift is about.

How do we operate this mindshift? How can we unlearn? The same way we learned. Step-by-step.

SELF-REFLECTION

Now that you have identified the mindtrap(s) that stand in your way, let's identify their origin.

1. **The voice of authority**
   - Which external voice can you associate with your mindtrap(s)?
   - Whose image or example do you see?

2. **The power of the collective**
   - Are you aware of the collective voices around you? How do they influence you?
   - How comfortable do you feel in your home, work, and social environments? Do you feel accepted for who you are? Or do you keep part of yourself hidden?

3. **Which voice do you listen to?**
   - Do you sometimes feel like the Native American elder with conflicting voices inside you? Which one do you feed?
   - Are you truly making your own choices and living your own life? Or do you often consider what someone else will say or think?
   - Is your idea of success truly your own or merely a race to keep up with the Joneses?

PART 2

Mindshift: Free Your Voice

In Part 1, we identified the mindtrap(s) that keep us from letting our own voice shine through. We've pulled them from the shadows and into the light of our consciousness. We can see their shape, why they emerged in the first place, and how they now keep us trapped. We understand whose voice they speak—a voice that is not our own.

Part 2 is about how to shift our mindtraps out of our way, so our path of roses emerges. How do we operate this mindshift? We do it in five steps. First by understanding how our brain can change and embrace a new perspective (Chapter 4), then by tapping into the empathy of others who see us from a different perspective (Chapter 5), and third by asking several simple but powerful questions to pull out the roots that our mindtraps have grown in our mind (Chapter 6). Step 4 is making the decision to let go of our mindtraps, as well as the voices and behaviors that go with them (Chapter 7). Only then can we take the fifth and final step: to sever the unconscious attachments associated with our mindtraps (Chapter 8).

With this mindshift, we create space for a truer, bigger, more authentic version of ourselves to emerge, which in turn transforms how we connect with ourselves and with others, becoming a human leader who shines a bright light in the world—the mindbuild covered in Part 3.

CHAPTER 4

How We Can Change Our Mindset

The Stories We Tell Ourselves

Still sitting by the fire in the old couple's hut, the child notices a painting hanging on the wall. The painting is of a beautiful beach at sunset.

"Where is that beach?" the child asks the old woman.

The old woman smiles. "Don't you recognize it?"

The child stares at the painting more closely and shakes his head.

"This is the beach by your village," the old woman says.

"This can't be," the child says. "On my beach, the sun never sinks into the water."

"Have you ever gone to your beach at sunset?" asks the old woman.

The child hasn't. But still, the beach on the painting doesn't look familiar. "There is no cliff on my beach," the child points out.

"Have you ever walked to the other side of your beach and looked from there?"

The child hasn't. But still, the beach on the drawing looks nothing like his. "My beach is much smaller," the child explains.

"Perhaps you've always gone at high tide," the old woman says.

Still, the child doesn't know the beach on the wall. "What about these waves?" the child asks, pointing at the painting. "On my beach, the ocean is flat."

"What happens when the wind blows?"

The child doesn't know. He stays home when the wind is strong.

"This is the same beach," says the old woman. "I often swam there when I was young. I used to walk to the far end, and from there, I could see the cliff. My best swimming was at sunset. The wind was up by then."

The child is dumbfounded. How can the exact same place look so different?

Then he notices the rain has stopped. It's time to go.

* * *

Before we embark on our mindshift, let's crack our heads open and look inside what Charles Darwin described as "the most important of all the organs." Why? Because understanding a few things about how our mind works is the first step toward changing it—which is what our mindshift is all about. And it is by fundamentally changing our mindset that we can transform how we lead.

Mindtraps are not the truths we believe they are. They are nothing more than stories we tell ourselves. We are, as author Jonathan Gottschall puts it, storytelling animals,[1] hardwired to tell ourselves—and each other—stories. We can't help it, as psychologists, Fritz Heider and Marianne Simmel already demonstrated in the 1940s. They showed 120 people a short animation of two triangles and a circle moving around. At the end, participants were asked about what they saw. Only three answered that they saw geometric forms moving around. Everyone else saw an intricate story involving human characters with personalities, emotions, and motives. For some, there was drama and romance. For others, comedy. Without even realizing it, they'd automatically created an elaborate human narrative where there was none. And even though they all watched the exact same animation, they each told a different story.[2]

Understanding why and how our brains automatically create these stories gives us the power to rewrite them. This is what this chapter is about. Humans are programmed to construct stories for two reasons:

- To organize into meaningful and memorable information the massive number of stimuli that bombard us
- To connect with each other

Why does this matter in our journey from superhero to human leader? Because the stories our brains automatically create greatly influence what we do and can achieve.

Finding Order in Chaos

First, our brains concoct stories to organize into meaningful and memorable information the massive number of stimuli that bombard us.

The three-pound mass in our skull that is our brain fits in the palms of our hands, but it is vastly complex and powerful. In fact, neuroscientist Paul MacLean saw it as three brains packaged into one. The reptilian brain is in charge of our survival instinct and other basic functions like eating, drinking, procreating, and fight or flight. The second brain, the limbic system, orchestrates our emotions. And the third brain—the neocortex—is home to our thoughts and rational thinking.

Our brain works as a gigantic network. Each of its roughly 100 billion cells, or neurons, connects to between 1,000 and 10,000 other neurons.[3] Neurons communicate with each other by shooting electric signals along these connections at lightning speed. Think of the busy megapolis in *The Fifth Element*, Luc Besson's 1997 movie, with its multitude of cars constantly flying on multiple levels through a vast network of highways, boulevards, streets, and small alleys connecting buildings and city blocks.

This complex machinery that is our brain has two main jobs. First, it is the command center that controls our body, our thoughts, and our emotions. Our brain's second main job is to "read" and make sense of our environment—including people—to identify threats and opportunities.

Big jobs for such a small organ! And it is for job number two that stories come in handy.

The Master Filter

Our senses are believed to send our brain an overwhelming 11 million or so pieces of information *every second.*[4] How can we possibly make sense of all this? Luckily, our brain is very efficient and helpful: it chooses the 40 or so that are most important at any given moment and leaves the rest out of our consciousness. In short, our brain shows us only a small corner of a gigantic puzzle. It creates a story that makes sense by assembling only the information relevant in that moment, so we can quickly assess and react to a situation.

I became aware of the brain's selective editing after I was attacked one evening while sitting in my car, stuck in traffic, as I mentioned in Chapter 2. When a thief broke the passenger window to steal my purse on the seat next to me, my awareness registered only the sound of glass breaking and a hand reaching into the car—just enough information for me to instinctively scream, duck the glass shards and recoil from the intrusive hand. When asked whether I'd seen the thief, I was convinced I hadn't. Only during hypnosis did I later realize that I had. My brain had captured everything, but a lot of information had been stored in my unconscious.

This filter is extraordinarily helpful: like a traffic cop, it makes sure we don't become gridlocked in a traffic jam of information. On the flipside, we're blissfully unaware of how much our brains mislead us. Because of this selective filter, we miss a lot of what's going on around us. In what has become one of the best-known experiments in psychology, Harvard researchers Christopher Chabris and Daniel Simons asked people to watch a short video in which six people—three wearing a black T-shirt and three wearing a white one—passed several basketballs around.[5]

Participants were asked to count how many times the players in white passed a ball. While viewers focus on multiple balls and players moving around, half of them miss a student dressed in a gorilla suit strolling among the players, thumping his chest for nine seconds, and then walking out of the frame. That sounds hard to believe, doesn't it? We all think that, surely, we couldn't miss something literally that big. Yet we do. All the time. This is one of the reasons why one person cannot possibly come up with all the answers.

The Meaning-Making Machine

In addition to filtering signals, our brain also interprets what they *mean* taken together. It makes connections and, whenever necessary, even fills in the blanks to create something that makes sense. In other words, it creates a story.

This is how our lives, what happens to us, what we hear and see, and our environment, all shape our brains and our mental patterns, largely out of our own awareness. Our human brains ask "why?" and, in their search for answers, make all kinds of associations and inferences, shaped by our experience and memories. Because our experience and memories are unique to each of us, what makes sense to you might not to another person.

If you'd like to visualize an extreme version of it, watch *The Good Doctor*. This TV drama offers a graphic representation of how the brain of surgical resident Shaun Murphy, who's been diagnosed with autism, searches the many textbooks and medical articles stored in his memory. It shows him making all kinds of lightspeed and complex links among them to find solutions to diagnostic or surgical problems that every other doctor finds intractable. This is how we find solutions to problems and also how we innovate: we link separate ideas or knowledge to create something new. Creating a work environment that supports and leverages that natural ability not only in ourselves but also in others is particularly helpful in times of extreme uncertainty or change like today. So, the human brain is a sort of Marie Kondo, the famous decluttering and organizing specialist. It automatically filters and organizes the avalanche of information to which we are exposed every day into patterns or stories that make sense and are helpful to us at a specific moment. And in these patterns or stories that we create, we find not only some order but also meaning. We can't help it. This is often how we see our lives: as a journey made of radically simplified and selective chains of events that are meaningful to us and linked together through cause and effect.

I remember the day when I coached my first client, for example. This felt like my calling. And suddenly, all the experiences and scenic detours I'd gone through in my life, which until then had seemed disconnected, made sense and came together. Step-by-step, they had collectively built the learning and experience I needed and led me to that moment. Apple founder Steve Jobs said it beautifully in his famous commencement address to Stanford graduates, in which he shared life lessons through personal stories: "You can't connect the dots looking forward; you can only connect them looking backwards."[6] Religions also rely heavily on stories to explain the world and establish moral values. So, our brains turn *everything* into stories.

We each filter, associate, and interpret these dots differently, however. If you ask my mother and me to describe our family holiday in the South of France when I was 12 years old, for example, you'll get very different answers. At any given time, our experiences, our memories, our personality, our mood—unique to each of us—all influence how we interpret and remember everything we perceive. Remember the experiment with the triangles and circle on the screen? People watched the same thing but they each saw a different story. So for my mother, our family holiday was a wonderful summer spent having fun, resting, eating good food, and enjoying the weather. But what I remember of that summer are long, boring, endless days.

Besides manufacturing meaning, our brain also transports us across past, present, and future, as well as great distances.

The Space and Time Traveler

Thanks to the stories our brain tells us, we can travel through space and time—all in our heads. In later chapters, we'll discuss how we can harness this ability to visualize and travel through space and time to transform ourselves. Close your eyes. Visualize yourself walking on your favorite beach. See the water. Can you hear the waves? Do you feel the sand under your bare feet, and the soft breeze brushing your skin? Or if I say "Darth Vader," a masked, black-clad villain will automatically spring to your mind, and you'll most likely hear heavy mechanical breathing and a gravelly voice—unless you've never watched *Star Wars*. During my family summer holiday, I escaped boredom by imagining I was around a campfire at the nearby camping ground, singing and dancing with friends my age.

These brain stories enable us to travel not only in space but also in time. French writer Marcel Proust famously described how biting into a madeleine unexpectedly filled him with a happiness that he initially could not place. After taking several bites, he suddenly remembered a long-forgotten memory. As a boy, he used to go into his aunt Leonie's bedroom to say hello every Sunday before mass. His aunt would then give him a small piece of madeleine dipped into her lime-blossom tea. Biting into the madeleine many years later unleashed a flood of happy feelings from his childhood. It also unearthed from his unconscious images of the entire town, with its square, streets, and gardens. If you've ever looked at old family photo albums or heard a song you haven't heard in a long time, you'll know that all our senses can be doors to our unconscious, bringing back to the surface memories and sensations.

Our brain's meaningful associations also enable us to travel into the future. As a child, designer Ralph Lauren dreamed of a better life. The child of Jewish immigrants of few means, he grew up sleeping three to a room. "I wanted to be a hero," he remembers, "a star, a somebody." He was too short to become a basketball player and thought he didn't have the looks of a movie star. But he loved the way Cary Grant and Frank Sinatra dressed. One day he would be just as stylish. He kept telling himself and whoever would listen the story of his future life. And this vision of a better life and of the American dream became central to the clothing and home lines he later designed and to the business he built.[7] Through visualizations, as Chapter 9 will illustrate, we too can create a blueprint of the future we want and find meaning in present challenges, creating an irresistible pull.

So, what's this universal and objective reality that we perceive all around us? There is no such thing, even though we're convinced there is. It is merely a construction of our brain—a story our brain makes for us out of selective filtering and interpretation—so we can make sense of our environment and our lives.

Why does it matter? It matters because it means that we are the director of our own movie! We can rewrite the stories our brains feed us about ourselves and our environment. In fact, we need to identify and edit some of these stories if we want to evolve, adapt, and change—including change how we lead.

Yet this filtering and meaning making is not the only reason our brain can't help but create stories. Stories are also how we read other people and connect to them.

The Human Connection

A crucial part of deciphering, filtering, and scanning our environment, one of our brain's main big jobs, is the human ability to read other people. This brain mechanism is meant to help us not only understand other people's motivation, feelings, and character but also anticipate how they will behave. For leaders, this is a powerful asset: we are, after all, social animals, whose impact greatly depends on collaborating with other humans. Tens of thousands of years ago, avoiding predators, finding enough to eat and drink, and finding shelter defined success. In our modern societies, success depends far more on our ability to influence and get along with others. Think of how crucial these skills are in most professional contexts, for example—whether you're part of a team, dealing with your company's board, or raising funds for a new venture. So our minds have sharpened their ability to become a lot more attuned to the minds of others.

But how do we do that? In two ways: by picking up external cues, and through our brain-to-brain connection.

The Gap Between Who We Are and How We Are Perceived

Imagine you're waiting in line at a coffee shop. When it's your turn, the cashier doesn't look at you and doesn't say hello. "What's your order?" he asks in a monotone, sullen voice. Then he gets your name and order wrong. What's your impression? Perhaps you think he's rude or bored. How come he still works here? you wonder. And so on. Now imagine that when it's your turn, the same cashier looks at you and greets you with a smile. "Good morning! How can I help you?" he says, like he truly means it. Here's someone in a good mood and with a positive attitude, you think. Someone who cares about customers. And you've already drawn some conclusions about him—and even about the coffee shop itself—weaving some sort of profile.

Without even thinking about it, we get cues from other people's facial expressions, their tone of voice, their body language, or even what they wear. We hear what they say and observe how they behave. Based on that information, and informed by our own experience and personality, our brains automatically draw quick conclusions on who they are—something known as "theory of mind." In fact, it takes one-tenth of a second for our brain to get a first impression and decide whether someone we've just met is competent, likable, trustworthy, aggressive, and attractive—just from their face.[8] This instinctive desire and ability to read others is at the heart of why we humans connect through stories.

Just like it does when assessing the environment, our brain makes shortcuts and inferences when reading people. What we gain in speed, we lose in accuracy, and we often misjudge other people's thoughts, feelings, and behavior. We read a stranger's thoughts and feelings accurately only about 20% of the time. And someone we know well? About a third of the time.[9] Humbling, isn't it? If this sounds incredibly low, ask yourself how often your spouse's or best friend's reactions to what someone said or did surprised you. And how often you've had an argument because of a misunderstanding.

All of us have experienced the gap between how others perceive us and who we feel we are. Anyone who has ever had a performance assessment or a 360 review knows that feeling. This is a gap that became very familiar to me when I left the corporate world and co-created a little business in the metal recycling industry. I knew nothing about chemistry or physics. In fact, I used to hate physics classes when I was at school— along with my physics teacher. In our company, I was the only non-engineer and the only woman. On a cold winter day, I went to a meeting with my business partner. The atmosphere felt as chilly as the weather: the four male engineers we were meeting took one look at me, and I could almost hear the unconscious chain of conclusions that led to their first impression: woman in a men's industry → non-engineer → brings no value → should not be here. After we shook hands, they didn't look at me and only spoke to my business partner, who was a scientist and spoke the same language they did. I might as well have been invisible. I stayed calm and listened carefully. Before the meeting ended, I asked a question. I must admit my heart was racing. "If my question is stupid," I thought, "I'll validate their bias." It turns out that my question raised a critical issue they had not thought about, and I could feel their initial perception of me shift in that moment. Suddenly they could see me! Like many of us, they had made a snap judgment—their brains had concocted a quick story—after taking one look at me. But the relevance and value of my question contradicted that initial narrative, so that story shifted, and in turn, their opinion.

So the story we tell ourselves about other people, and the story they create about us both shape how we relate to each other. Yet they are often inaccurate. But realizing it is a "story" gives us the power to change it.

The "Gandhi Neurons"

Besides constructing stories to read people, our brains also help us connect with each other through stories. For the social animals that we are, this human connection is instinctive and vital, and our neurons are engineered to help us do this. Imagine you're cycling. Brain cells known as your motor neurons send pedaling signals to your legs and, when needed, braking signals to your hands. But if you merely *see* someone else cycling, a subset of these brain cells—roughly 20%—will get activated in exactly the same way as if you were cycling yourself. The same is true not only for movement but also for experiences like touch or pain. Part of your brain mirrors someone else's brain.

This is all very interesting, but what does it have to do with stories and human connections? And why should you care? Mirror neurons matter for two reasons. First, they make us able to imitate—or mirror—others. This is crucial for learning. Any mother and father spooning vegetable puree to a baby, for example, open their mouth without thinking to encourage their six-month-old to do the same. Mirror neurons underscore how leaders can become role models and influence others, their actions reverberating in the mind of others like sound waves. Second, some neurologists believe that mirror neurons give us the ability to stand in someone else's shoes—in short, empathize with other human beings. This is why Neurologist V. S. Ramachandran calls mirror neurons "Gandhi neurons."[10] In the late 19th century, German philosopher Robert Vischer first coined the word *Einfühlung*—literally "to feel within"—to describe how viewers could understand artwork by projecting onto it and internalizing its emotional significance. This was later understood as empathy, or the ability to understand and share others' feelings.

Stories crank up the intensity of this connection. When you listen to someone telling you a story, your brain is activated in the same places and in the same way as the storyteller's. This usually happens with a slight delay, as you absorb and comprehend the information your interlocutor has shared with you. But even more extraordinary, your brain activity sometimes *precedes* the storyteller's, when you anticipate and predict what's coming. And the more you understand the story, the more your brain syncs with the other person.[11] When the story is emotional, then your brain reacts by activating areas involved in processing emotions.[12]

Through a well-told story—a book, a film, or simply something someone tells you—we feel what the character feels. Even if the story is not real, or is happening to someone else, your unconscious perceives it as if it is happening to you, and your body reacts accordingly. If you've ever watched a horror movie or a fast-paced thriller, you know exactly what I mean. You know the story is not real; yet you feel adrenalin rush through your veins, almost as if you were being chased down a dark alley by an axe murderer instead of sitting in your living room. A good cliffhanger? Off goes our dopamine, which keeps us engaged and curious, so we want to know more. Emotional stories trigger the release of oxytocin, which activates our sense of empathy: we share the emotions of the characters. This emotional connection opens the door to a change of perspective. By featuring two charming and funny gay men as its main characters, for example, popular TV show *Will and Grace* significantly reduced homophobia.[13] Our storytelling brains even project a human personality onto our favorite pets or inanimate objects—anyone who's ever nicknamed their car or felt during a game of poker that the cards didn't like them will understand what I mean. This is why stories are powerful tools for leaders to engage, convince, and motivate others, as well as an instrument of change—including to change ourselves.

So like trees in a forest are all connected via an invisible underground fungal network, our human brains are able to connect directly with each other. We now understand why and how our attitude, mood, beliefs, and behavior can influence people around us, but also why and how theirs influence us. Have you noticed how being around positive people helps lift your mood? What happens when you feel low, and you watch a funny movie or listen to upbeat music? I remember one trip years ago when I flew from Paris to visit my daughter who was studying in Montreal. After I landed, I was feeling tired and jetlagged, but my daughter couldn't wait to shop with her mother, so we went to a few stores. Everywhere, I was greeted at the door with smiles and "how are you feeling today?" My energy and spirit quickly lifted, and I realized how much we can influence others' mood, outlook, and well-being just through our own attitude. It struck me that this was a crucial part of my leadership role in the venture I'd co-created: by remaining authentically optimistic and positive, I could greatly influence the collective mood and generate positive energy throughout the organization.

Conversely, you've perhaps noticed that it is harder and takes energy to stay upbeat when everyone around you is struggling. During the COVID-19 pandemic, for example, even people who did not directly suffer the loss of a loved one or worry about their jobs found it more difficult to stay positive, because they felt the stress and grief that many people around them experienced and reacted to stories on the news. More generally, the string of bad news we typically get from the media, from natural disasters, wars, and terrorist attacks to economic challenges, directly affects us. Whether we want it or not, our brains absorb collective sentiments and opinions, particularly from people we care about, admire, or identify with. Over time, these opinions and sentiments solidify as truth—about the world, about ourselves, and about other people.

* * *

Now, we know why telling ourselves and each other stories is a biological imperative. It is through stories that we not only make sense of our environment and our life but also best read, connect with, and influence each other. We can't help it, even if we try. The stories we tell both ourselves and each other shape how we see ourselves, others, and the world—our attitudes, our outlooks, and our beliefs, including our mindtraps.

The good news is, because these mindtraps are only stories that our brains have concocted, we have the power to change them. Why does this matter? It matters greatly, because by rewriting the stories that are our attitudes, outlooks, and beliefs, we can influence our results. This is the core of football coach Ted Lasso's approach in the TV show of the same name. One of the first things he does as a new coach is to step into the locker room and stick a handwritten poster on the wall that reads "Believe." Believe in the vision. Believe in everyone's potential. Believe in yourself. Mindtraps rob us of this belief in what's possible.

When studying statistics at UC Berkeley in the 1930s, mathematician George Dandzig arrived late for class one day. He saw two problems on the blackboard, which he assumed were homework. Feeling they were a little harder than usual, it took him a few days to solve them. Only when his excited teacher banged on his door did he learn that what he thought was homework were in fact two of the most famous unsolved statistical problems.[14] Had he expected these problems to be unsolvable, the outcome might have been different.

Just like our lives shape our brains through our experience, our brains in turn shape our lives. What we believe is possible influences the outcome. And this plays a fundamental role in any change we want to make, particularly when it comes to changing ourselves.

So if you want to change your outcomes, first examine your beliefs. And if you want to change how you lead, then shift your mindtraps out of the way. Your perspectives and mindset, especially those we've been nurturing for a long time, may be deep-seated, but they are not set in stone. Our brain and our neural connections change. Unused pathways disappear and new ones are made.

This is what the mindshift described in the following chapters is all about.

SELF-REFLECTION

1. Finding order in chaos

- How sure are you that you see the big picture? Are you aware of how much you miss?
- How do you see the story of your life so far? In your view, what are its most meaningful events and how are they connected (if they are)?

2. The human connection

- Does what makes sense and is meaningful to you also do the same thing for your family, your peers, your team?
- What is the biggest gap between how you view yourself and how others view you?
- Are you aware of your emotions and of how they influence people around you?
- Are you attuned to the emotions of people around you? How do they influence yours?
- Who gives you energy and joy? Who drains you? Why?

CHAPTER 5

See Yourself Differently

A View from Outside the Frame

The child bids the old couple farewell and continues his walk through the forest. After a while, he comes across a quiet pond next to a cave. The child sits by the water to rest, sheltering in the cave.

"How am I going to find the path of roses?" he wonders out loud. "Who will show me the way?"

"You can find it," the cave echoes in the child's own voice.

"But I have no map!" the child says.

"All you have to do is look inside your heart," the voice answers.

The child reflects for a moment. "How can I see inside my own heart?" the child asks. "My eyes look only outward." He leans over the pond and sees his own image looking back at him. The image looks pure and radiant.

"I can see your heart clearly from here," says the image in the water, "and the map is already there. I will help you find it."

* * *

Knowing that we can shift our mindtraps sets us on the road to do so. Yet often, there is only so far we can go by ourselves. We typically need an external trigger or an outside perspective—sometimes both—to help us engineer a mindshift. This chapter examines the following questions:

- Why can crises trigger a mindshift?
- How can external perspectives help us?
- How do we open our eyes, ears, and mind?

Hitting the Wall

A crisis—what former Medtronic CEO and author Bill George calls a *crucible*—can open our eyes and nudge us to change if we are willing to learn from it.

When he was 32 years old, Doug Conant abruptly lost what he describes as "the best job in the world"—director of marketing for a toy and games company. One morning he turned up at work and was told that his job had been eliminated. He had until noon to pack his things and go home. He was stunned. How could this happen to him? That life—a job he loved, which had brought him and his young family to a small town in Massachusetts— was meant to be, he thought. What was he going to do? He felt like his career and his life were over. But he had not yet realized that this was the first day of a personal transformation, as we'll see later in this chapter, that eventually led him to become chief executive of Campbell Soup Company and other iconic businesses.[1]

Crucibles come in many different shapes. And when it comes to mindtraps we've been unable to see or unwilling to address, our bodies often raise the alarm. Professional basketball player Kevin Love, for example, felt his heart rate go out of control during a game against the Hawks a few years ago. Suddenly, he was struggling to catch his breath, and everything was spinning. He had to leave the court in the middle of the game and ended up on the floor of the locker room, unable to breathe. After a visit to the clinic, he understood that he'd had a full-blown panic attack, after ignoring and repressing depression and anxiety for his entire life. He immediately worried that this would become public. And this was his wake-up call: if he wanted to keep playing basketball, he could no longer bottle up his emotions or live in fear that, if someone found out he'd had a panic attack, they might think him weird or weak, or worse, it might ruin his career. He realized he needed help.[2]

Embarking on a mindshift does not have to be so dramatic, however. An external perspective, sometimes from a few words, a book, or a movie that resonates, or the example of someone else that inspires us, can also make us realize not only that we've been stuck but also that it's time to get unstuck.

The Gift of External Perspective

Top classical musicians are very different from top athletes in many ways. Perhaps the most striking is how they approach their craft. Athletes do not believe they can reach and maintain top performance on their own, so every Roger Federer or Usain Bolt has a coach. Musicians, however, train to reach a level of mastery after which they're typically expected to no longer need instruction. They get into a prestigious program like Julliard, spend years practicing technique, learning discipline, mastering a broad repertoire and fine-tuning performance. Then they graduate and are supposed to spend the rest of their lives refining their skills by themselves.

Among world-class violinists, Itzhak Perlman is an exception. For the past several decades, he's relied on his wife, Toby, to help him refine his playing. "The great challenge in performing is listening to yourself," he says. No matter how hard they try, performers cannot hear what the audience does. His wife is his outside ear, helping him play better.[3]

Outside ears, eyes and minds are invaluable to anyone wanting to be the best they can at anything—including becoming a different kind of leader. Why? Because it is a lot easier to see the picture when you're not in the frame. We all have blind spots about ourselves and find it easier to see the speck in someone else's eye than the plank in our own. As discussed previously in this book, we don't know our own selves and how we come across to others as well as we think we do. We are so used to our own perspective that often we cannot see what's getting in our way.

And there is no tape of life that we can watch the way athletes do after a game.

This is where an outside perspective can help. When it comes to seeing a mindtrap at work—these beliefs and perspectives that have become obstacles—and shifting it out of the way, a bit of distance often provides a better view. Where can we find that external perspective to help us with our mindshift? We typically find it in three places:

- In our immediate environment
- From stories
- From professional guides

Your Immediate Environment

People closest to us are well positioned to see—and say—when a mindtrap is at work. "You know what I think you should do? Just have fun!" This is the advice Yasmin Brunet gave to surfing champion Gabriel Medina, who was also her husband, a few minutes before Australia's 2021 competition in Narrabeen. The competition would determine who would be surfing world champion that year, and a lot had been weighing on Gabriel's mind. He'd lost to rival Italo Ferreira, the reigning world champion, only one week earlier. For the first time in his life, he was traveling and competing without his stepdad, who had given him his first surfboard as a boy and had been his coach ever since. Following a family rift, he was working with a new coach. He wanted to know whether he could regain his world title without his stepdad. He also wanted to show that getting married wouldn't distract him and destroy his career. He'd stepped into the unknown, and his wife could see that it was weighing on his mind, obscuring the joy and lightness of riding waves.

Medina won that day, reaching new heights with a surfing performance that blew everyone's mind. Judges and commentators noticed how much he was enjoying himself, his love of surfing shining through. "I was going through a hard moment, and the only way to get out the best stuff was being happy," Medina explained afterwards.[4]

In my case, both a close friend and members of a professional group showed me what I could not see. I still remember talking to a close friend while driving in Paris, at a time when I hadn't yet accepted how profoundly misaligned I was in my marriage and in the corporate world. "Why do you keep finding excuses for everyone but yourself?" he blurted out. I was speechless. At the same time, his words resonated profoundly. He was right! I'd been finding excuses to keep a self-destructive status quo. I had indeed forgotten who I was. On the surface, I had a good job and a wonderful family. In reality, I was living in a golden cage: little by little, I had lost my self-esteem and confidence. This one sentence, spoken from an external perspective, shocked me out of my emotional coma. How could I have been so blind? I understood for the first time that I had to make radical changes in my professional and personal life.

It took me a while to become ready to act and start over. When I left my marriage and my corporate job, I felt I could finally breathe! I'd been dying slowly, and I wanted to live. But I was terrified and had no idea what to do next, so I joined a workshop to help me think about it. The workshop leader asked the 15 participants to describe who we were, what we'd done so far, and our skills. My first thought was: *I have no particular skill!* But I got over my nerves and went through the exercise, describing my jobs in marketing and ad sales. I then concluded by saying that I wasn't sure what my specific skills were. Then every other participant had to repeat in their own words what they'd heard, their impression, and what they thought I could do. I expected some embarrassing feedback, but to my surprise, they saw a version of myself that I couldn't see: someone independent, creative, who easily connects with people, and has valuable marketing skills. The gap between their perspective and my own couldn't have been wider. Seeing myself through their eyes revealed that

I was locked into a self-doubt mindtrap that stopped me from moving forward.

The other participants then helped me uncover my aspirations and talents, which resuscitated some of my confidence and enthusiasm. "You should start your own business!" they all suggested. I knew that I cherished my own freedom, but locked as I was into my mindtrap, I'd stopped allowing myself to think I could ever be an entrepreneur. The external perspective and support that the workshop provided started a mindshift, giving me the energy and confidence I needed to consider a different future—one full of possibilities. The workshop leader also introduced me to research on the human mind and techniques that further opened my eyes on how I could change my outlook, all of which I found fascinating. By the end of the program several weeks later, I'd come up with an idea for a business that I was excited about. While exploring it, I then met the man who would later become my business partner. This workshop was a decisive *aha* moment, which shifted my perspective and was the first step toward uncovering who I really was and living my life accordingly.

Watching someone else's behavior and actions can also help shift our own by providing a powerful alternative perspective and mindset. For Microsoft CEO Satya Nadella, for instance, that someone else was his wife. When their first son was born with cerebral palsy, Satya Nadella's life changed. All the plans and thoughts he'd had went out of the window. *Why is this happening to me?* he initially thought. His wife, however, adopted an entirely different attitude. From the moment she recovered from the birth, she decided she wouldn't go back to work and instead drove their son to every possible therapy to give him the best chance she could.

Watching her naturally care and connect with their son over the following couple of years, Satya Nadella then realized that nothing had happened to *him*; instead, something had happened to their son. This mindshift enabled him to see the world through the perspective of his child. "As I figured it out, it changed me, both obviously as a parent, but also who I am today and how I approach everything," he says. He credits this change for teaching him the importance of empathy, which he considers essential to business success, and has transformed the way he leads. He argues that to innovate and be successful, businesses must see the world from their customers' perspective, so they can understand and meet their needs, even when unarticulated.[5] This perspective was essential to transform the culture and trajectory of Microsoft, which, before he became CEO, had missed the shifts toward cloud and mobile computing and was losing its edge.

More generally, there is great value in considering external perspectives to help us widen or shift our own—what writer Napoleon Hill labeled a *mastermind alliance.* Between 1915 and 1924, industrialists Henry Ford and Harvey Firestone, together with naturalist John Burroughs and inventor Thomas Edison, famously embarked on summer camping trips,[6] during which they exchanged ideas and learned from each other. One of my clients, the CEO of a nonprofit organization, came to consider her organization's board of directors as a mastermind alliance of sorts, whose role was to support her by offering ideas and perspectives different from her own.

The Power of Words

Friends, family, and peers are not the only source of external perspective. Good books, movies, plays, talks, or podcasts too can help trigger some awareness and help shift our mindset. Have you ever felt that words on a page, on screen, on stage, or coming through your earphones profoundly resonate within you? Although these words are spoken by a stranger or a fictitious character, they feel like they are specifically meant for you. Suddenly, you can see clearly something that had so far been obscured or incomprehensible, which deepens your understanding of yourself, others, or the world. I once attended a talk with actor, singer, dancer, director, and choreographer André De Shields, who was awarded Tony and Grammy awards for the role of Hermes in the Broadway musical *Hadestown*. He explained that every time he's on stage, his mission is to deliver a message to the audience. I wondered how many spectators he's helped over the years through a story, dialogue, or character in which they recognized themselves and which helped them shift a mindtrap.

I've experienced this feeling firsthand. I still remember how reading Paramahansa Yogananda's autobiography profoundly resonated with me, for example. The Indian spiritual leader and yogi was sent abroad as a young man by his spiritual master, and this exposure later helped him introduce yoga and Eastern spirituality to the United States. What first struck me from his story was how his yogi master guided him toward knowledge, confidence, and wisdom, which then broadened my perspective to other forms of learning and spirituality. Also, his sense of purpose profoundly inspired me. What if I, too, could find my own sense of mission in life? I was so inspired that I decided to find a yogi master aligned with Paramahansa Yogananda's spirit and journey—not an easy task in a place like Paris. I asked and researched for months until I found the right guide. Krishna Patel introduced me to Indian philosophy, spirituality, and meditation, and my work with him helped me reconnect with myself and find a sense of purpose. At the same time, I realized that I'd done and learned more than I thought during my journey. Sharing what I'd learned could help others, I thought, which led me to coaching. And it all started with a story in a book that struck a chord deep inside me.

Books, plays, and movies can also reveal that it is time to offload unacknowledged baggage. Watching the movie adaptation of Elizabeth Gilbert's *Eat, Pray, Love* turned out to be another, even if smaller, *aha* moment. When the main character realizes that she has yet to forgive herself for leaving her husband, I felt like I'd been punched in the stomach. This helped me see that I, too, had been carrying a crippling and unacknowledged sense of guilt toward my children, which was weighing me down.

Many years ago, a friend of mine picked up neuropsychiatrist Louann Brizendine's book on the female brain at an airport bookstore before a flight. She devoured it in one seating and almost felt her neural pathways shift and reorganize on every page.[7] Within a few hours, her perspective had completely shifted: all the traits that for so long she'd considered as unimportant or as personal character weaknesses to be corrected, such as her ability to "read" people and the room around her, connect with others' emotions or seek consensus, were in fact natural for most women and could be wonderful assets. This was life changing: she finally felt "normal"! The problem, she concluded, wasn't her, but rather a corporate environment that structurally favored and promoted behavior and traits most often found in men, such as overconfidence and being comfortable with confrontation.

Crises and external perspectives can therefore help us see and shift our mindtraps. The examples just described illustrate that, if we pay close attention, these alternative perspectives can be found in many places and in many people.

Yet it is much easier to travel from mindtrap to mindshift and mindbuild with the sustained help of a skilled and trusted guide.

The Professional Guide

After Doug Conant was told he no longer had a job as marketing director of the toy and games company, he went home, devastated and feeling like a victim. Later that day, the head of human resources called to connect him with an outplacement counselor. When the counselor called, Doug Conant swore at him and slammed the phone down. A few hours later, however, he decided to call him back. What happened next changed the course of his life.

After they talked for three hours, his counselor asked him to write his life story—by hand. He had to include everything he remembered, big and small. Doug Conant was initially skeptical. How would this help him find another job? But the counselor argued that, if he wanted to step forward, he first had to take a step back. So for the following two weeks, Conant handwrote 50 pages in small cursive. After he handed it in, his counselor helped him realize that there seemed to be two different people: the Doug Conant who was in front of him—eager to fit in—and the Doug Conant who transpired through the pages he'd written— ferociously competitive and who wanted to make a difference in the world. Reflecting on it now, Conant is shocked by how much writing these 50 pages taught him. "I was walking in someone else's story," he says—a story that other people had written for him. With the help of his counselor, he started developing his own convictions, instead of what his parents or teachers believed or thought, and, in his own words, "looking for his own story."[8]

To help you identify a mindtrap, operate a mindshift, and then engineer a mindbuild to become an effective human leader, a guide—whether a coach, a counselor, or a spiritual teacher— should ideally have three main qualities:

- They must genuinely want to help you, care about you, and believe in you.
- They must also be able to connect with what you're feeling and thinking, mirror it back to you effectively and honestly, and help you connect some dots to interpret what it all means.
- They must have the ability to do all this without judgment and setting aside their own emotions, beliefs, and history.

How can you determine whether someone meets the first criterion? Here are a few clues. Do you feel they listen to you carefully, or talk too much, trying to impress you? Do they ask questions about you, your goals, and who you are, and do they seem genuinely interested in your answers? How did you feel after your first meeting? Energized or discouraged? Inspired or lost? Sad or happy? Confident or skeptical?

Now, about the second quality: an effective guide must be able to help you connect some dots. Doug Conant's counselor, for instance, helped him understand that he was not being his true self. How? By having him write his life story. As I mentioned, I, too, sought help from a professional guide—a yogi master—who helped me find a sense of purpose in my life. Every guide is different, each with his or her own approach, style, and bag of tools. You need to find the right one for you.

Effectively guiding others, however, also requires the ability to connect with what they're feeling and thinking—or empathy. During my coaching conversations, for example, I fully open my eyes, my ears, and my heart. A subtle change of voice, a minute facial expression, eyes changing directions or a small shift in breathing are all clues that are like breadcrumbs showing me the path to follow to help identify and shift a mindtrap. Our body language sends subtle and often unconscious cues that reflect our true emotions and state of mind, which we're not always aware of. If you've been around horses, for instance, you probably know that they have an uncanny ability to perceive these subtle cues and instinctively mirror any whiff of confusion, shaky confidence, or emotional turmoil they perceive in their handlers. They are the ultimate empaths. In fact, some coaches help leaders learn to build relationships, emotional intelligence, and self-awareness by having them work with horses (more on this in Chapter 11).

When looking for mindtraps and then working to defuse them with external eyes and ears in the room, we also flex our mirror neurons, which enables us to feel what others are feeling—in short, to empathize—and recognize others' emotions and intentions by matching their brain activity. This is what happens when I'm in coaching mode and attuned to my clients. Thanks to this brain-to-brain connection, I can feel somebody else's emotions in my own body, which helps me understand when and why they are stuck and guide them to shift their mindtrap. When a client recently told me about his life after he and his wife had children, for example, I felt an emptiness and sadness in my chest. I knew these emotions belonged to him and I understood that, amidst the busy day-to-day life, he'd lost the close connection he'd previously enjoyed with his wife, which had been a great source of energy for him.

The ability to remove oneself, however, is just as essential as the ability to step into someone else's world, connect with their feelings, and profoundly understand them. An effective guide cannot help anyone if they get lost in other people's feelings. An effective guide must maintain an external perspective—and be like Yitzhak Perlman's outside ear.

Helping someone connect some dots to see and shift their mind-trap also requires effective and honest communication, whichever form this may take. Everyone has their own style. Legendary coach and business executive Bill Campbell, who mentored countless tech entrepreneurs and executives, liked to say, "This is the sound of your head coming out of your ass." He was famous for his unique and blunt ways, and other "Billisms" included "You're so fucked up you make *me* look good" and "You're as dumb as a post." But no one ever doubted how deeply he cared about people and about helping them.[9] Whether or not this is your style of honesty, any effective guide must help you see what you don't.

What of quality number three? To be effective, a guide must be like a camera that captures and projects a clear picture, not one that distorts shapes and colors by applying a filter. One's own emotions, history, and beliefs are like a camera filter, and they're not helpful when guiding someone else to find their own path. When I step into my coaching role, for instance, I prepare myself not only by going over my notes but also by emptying my mind so I can listen, watch, and become fully attuned to my clients' thoughts and emotions while leaving my own out of the room.

Yet an external perspective—whether from someone close to you, a story, or a professional guide—can help shift your mind-trap only if you're ready and able to change.

Open Your Ears, Eyes, and Mind

Getting an external perspective to help you shift a mindtrap requires opening up to someone you trust and a willingness to revisit your own perspective. Do you confide in anyone—whether a coach, a friend, a relative, a mentor, or a colleague? Do you have an emotional support system? A recent survey highlights the rise of loneliness, particularly among US men, who have fewer and fewer close friends and are often raised in a way that does not encourage emotional connection in male friendship.[10] At the minimum, it means being open to, and seeking, different perspectives. We can all gain a fresh outlook from a book, a movie, or a TED Talk *only if* we are open to challenging our mindset.

To benefit from an external perspective, we also must be willing to hear and take on board what might be uncomfortable truths. Remember Bill George, the former CEO of Medtronic, and the epiphany he had in his car one day driving near his home? He realized that the power, glory, and status he had been pursuing were in fact making him miserable because he couldn't be himself. He had to stop trying so hard to become the CEO of Honeywell and instead adopt a style of leadership focused on his own values. When he got home, he told his wife, Penny. "I've been trying to tell you this for a year," she told him, "but you weren't prepared to hear it."[11] Do you remember the experiment mentioned in Chapter 4 during which participants failed to see a gorilla walking among basketball players? Unless we broaden our focus and pay attention, it is easy to miss the signals and alternative perspectives that are all around us.

Conversely, it was former Ford CEO Alan Mulally's willingness and ability to listen to feedback that proved decisive in shifting his mindtrap and transforming his leadership style. When he first became a supervisor early in his career at Boeing, he was to sign off on a young engineer's coordination sheet, which documented his technical work. When Mulally got the first draft, he marked it up and sent it back with some feedback and suggestions. Then came a revised draft, on which Mulally enthusiastically offered more comments. By the 13th version, the young engineer told Mulally he'd had enough and was leaving.

"You're quitting?" asked a stunned Mulally. "Why?"

The engineer told him he could no longer stand being micromanaged. The first couple rounds of feedback were great, he added, but they were now way past the point of diminishing returns.

"What do you think I should do?" asked Mulally.

The young engineer suggested he might want to consider sharing the vision and the plan for the airplane program, maybe ask whether he had the right people and the right tools, and then nurture that environment.

"That sounds useful," Mulally replied. "If I do those things, will you stay?"

"Absolutely not," said the engineer.

Mulally says that this was a life-changing event for him. He stayed in touch with his former report, so he could prove to him that he'd changed his approach.

Another watershed moment was when the pilots in the airplane program came to see him on a Sunday. "This is not who you are as a person," they told him. "And that's not what we need going forward." They were talking about the command-and-control approach that characterized the Boeing corporate environment at the time, and that Alan Mulally had been absorbing. He had to decide whether to move to a far more participatory style focused on coaching, nurturing, and facilitating, or they would quit the program. His openness to feedback made him realize he had to change.[12]

Being prepared to hear uncomfortable truths and then act takes courage. Take businesswoman Gail Miller, who chairs the LHM group of companies in Utah. After getting married to her husband, Larry, she focused on raising their five children while Larry started and built a phenomenally successful family business. The problem was she gradually felt more and more disconnected from the world, silently wilting away as the confidence that her upbringing had given her was gradually evaporating. "I actually felt invisible, because whenever I would go anywhere with my husband, he would be the one that would be recognized," she says. "And I'd be standing there, and no one would even acknowledge me." Until one day when she took one of her young children to see a therapist. "I'm happy to help your child," the therapist told her. "But you're the one who needs help." She could easily have dismissed the therapist's words. Instead, she clearly heard them and used them as a firing rod. She decided to work on rebuilding her confidence, recovering her sense of self, and broadening her horizons. It wasn't easy, and it took time. But had she not been open to that feedback, she might not have been equipped to step in and successfully take the reins of the family business after her husband died.

* * *

If we open our eyes, ears, and minds, a trigger—a crisis or an external perspective that touches a nerve or resonates—can help set in motion a mindshift. Chapter 6 deepens our mindshift by asking key questions to uproot the mindtraps standing in the way of our inner human leader.

SELF-REFLECTION

1. Hitting the wall
- Think about difficult moments in your life. Did they change, or are they changing, your perspective about your-self, others, or the world?

2. The gift of external perspective
- Has a family member, a friend, or a colleague ever said something that made you question your own perspective on yourself?

- Do you remember reading a book or watching a movie or a play that resonated so deeply that it completely shifted your perspective?
- Have you ever worked or considered working with a coach, a counselor, or a guide?
- Whom do you ask for advice?

3. Open your ears, eyes, and mind

- Be aware of any words or situations that resonate with you. Do you understand why they feel so relevant?

CHAPTER 6

Challenge Your Beliefs

Is It True, Relevant, or Helpful Today?

After the child leaves the pond next to the cave, he comes across a goblin. The goblin looks friendly, so the child shares his conundrum: he's searching for the path of roses, but he's not sure what to think of the foreign-princess-on-a-horse story anymore.

"Do you have legs?" the goblin then asks.

"Yes," says the child.

"Do you have eyes and ears?"

Yes and yes.

"Do you know how to use them?"

The child nods, perplexed.

"Do you know this forest?"

Better than anyone, the child says. He lives in the village nearby and he often plays there or collects mushrooms.

"Last I heard, the foreign princess has only two eyes and two ears and two legs, just like you. But unlike you, she doesn't know this area. So how can it be true that only she can show you the way?" asks the goblin. "In any case, even if it were true, it wouldn't matter."

"Why not?" the child asks.

"Because I've never seen any foreign princess around here. So how does that help you?"

* * *

Once we've identified our mindtraps and the individual or collective voices associated with them, understood that they're only stories that our brain has created, and perhaps gotten an external nudge to embark on a mindshift, how do we break free? Unearthing these voices from our unconscious and bringing them into our awareness already drains some of the power they hold over our mind—just like sunlight neutralizes germs that would otherwise fester in the dark. So being aware of our mindtraps and the voice—or voices—that feed them is a good start.

Yet it's often not enough. To operate a mindshift, we must challenge these voices head on and make space for our own voice and perspective to emerge. How do we challenge the voices and create that mental space? By working our way through several critical questions:

- Is it true?
- Is it relevant?
- Is it still helpful?

These are deceptively simple but powerful questions that shine an even brighter light onto the external voices that we carry with us, thereby further loosening their grip on our mind and our actions.

Truth Be Told

To answer the first question, we must decide whether our mindtrap is grounded in our reality today or whether evidence suggests there is space for an alternative perspective.

Claire

"Is it true?" I asked Claire. We were working first on her mother's voice, who'd told her she was messy and disorganized, as well as insane. "Is your home untidy?"

"Not particularly," she said. "But it's not always perfectly tidy, either."

I pointed out that she had three young children. Claire laughed and admitted that, seen in that context, the house was fine.

"What about your current job, and the one you had before? Do you regularly miss deadlines? Or is your team confused?"

"No," said Claire.

If anything, she was very much "in control," following a strict routine of swimming pool laps for one hour every day before heading to the office, then working hard, and spending time with her husband and children in the evenings.

"What does 'insane' mean to you?" I went on.

Claire thought for a moment. "'Insane' means being ill and out of control."

"Is there anything in your life suggesting you're ill and out of control?"

Claire confirmed there wasn't. She had a job, she was happily married, and she loved her children.

Would she have been offered the job she had if there was something remotely wrong with her? No.

What about her father's "voice" and his idea of success, which made Claire believe that she wasn't good enough? Yes, her father had reached the highest echelons of business, with a prestigious job heading a large company and multiple public accolades. And from Claire's perspective, because she hadn't achieved similar public recognition and she wasn't a CEO, she was a failure. Never mind that the nature of her job, which was about communication, didn't lend itself to the kind of hard targets, job titles, or glorifying media profiles that her father had in mind when he talked about "results." Never mind that, because her job involved ruffling some feathers by disrupting the status quo within her company, it would take time before some of her colleagues acknowledged the value of what she was doing. And never mind that the CEO of her current company had identified her as perfect for the position and convinced her to leave her previous job. That her career didn't look like her father's was all she'd been able to see.

"Do you think your boss is a failure?" I asked.

"No!" she exclaimed. In fact, he was probably pretty close to what Claire's father would have considered successful.

"Do you trust his judgment?"

Claire did.

"So, if a successful CEO with good judgment has head-hunted you for this job because he thinks you're exactly what the company needs, how can you be a failure?"

It was time to put another aspect of her father's voice to the truth test: Did she genuinely agree with her father's idea of success? To find out, I asked her to write her own eulogy, including several perspectives—her family's, her friends', and her colleagues'. How did she want to be remembered? What would she want people to say about her at the end of her life? These questions are an excellent measure of what we truly value and what is most important to us. As such, they can reveal a disconnect with perspectives we've been holding but that don't belong to us—like they did in Claire's case.

A few days later, when I read what she'd written, none of it was about the results, public accolades, and big titles that she'd been associating with success. Claire wanted her family, friends, and colleagues to remember her as someone who listened to them, understood them, and helped them in times of need. She wanted to be remembered as someone who cared deeply about others—whether her spouse, her children, her friends, or her colleagues—and made a difference in their lives. Ultimately, a successful life, for her, was all about the emotional intelligence that both her parents had dismissed as a complete waste of time.

To strengthen the inner voice that was starting to emerge in Claire's mind, I suggested she ask her friends to share with her what her best qualities were. Claire was stunned to hear them say with no hesitation how funny and intelligent she was, and how she was always there for them. But what about her colleagues? We reviewed together the feedback she'd received from her team in her previous job. "Excellent leader," "caring," and "really like working with her" were the most frequent descriptions. She'd dismissed and forgotten anything good they'd had to say about her, because these weren't the kind of "results" she'd so far associated with success. This filter had kept her self-esteem and her energy down.

A short time later, she arrived for one of our coaching sessions with a spring in her step and a smile on her face. "I just went to a work conference," she said, very excited. "People kept on talking about this thing, and I felt every time they spoke about it, they were talking about me! They called it EQ." I smiled. I was so happy Claire had realized that EQ—short for emotional quotient, also known as emotional intelligence—was not a waste of time after all, but a critical asset, not only at home but also at work. And this was a kind of intelligence that, along with the more traditional IQ, she possessed in droves but hadn't dared deploy fully in her professional life, convinced as she'd been that it was unimportant. Once Claire had recognized how her parents' voices had kept her trapped, she could start reclaiming the power they had over her.

Andrew

Measuring whether someone else's voice, once identified, is true for you is sometimes much easier. Take Andrew, the top executive who was vying for the job of group CEO, until the trauma of an oral exam many years earlier got in the way. It was easy for him to realize that his professor's prediction—that he'd never become CEO because he was too obviously emotional—wasn't an absolute truth, but merely an opinion that Andrew could choose to disagree with. First, Andrew was already heading one of the group's subsidiaries, so although he wasn't chosen to become the CEO of the group, he'd already proven his professor wrong. In any case, even if some CEOs indeed fit the picture his professor had painted—the all-knowing and unflappable superhero leader—Andrew knew of successful CEOs and top executives who were unafraid to embrace their emotions, humanity, and empathy, and to genuinely connect with people. This was a style of leadership that Andrew instinctively felt far more comfortable with. Finally, he was no longer the young and impressionable student that had absorbed his professor's words at face value. His older self was far more easily able to distance himself from his mindtrap and make space for his own voice and opinion.

Hortense

What of collective voices, however? How can we create distance from such a pervasive influence? How can we hang on to another perspective in the face of an overwhelming collective view? By finding voices and examples that belie collective norms. Chapter 3, for example, relates how a teenage Arianna Huffington had chosen to listen to her mother's voice as well as her own to believe she could study at Cambridge one day, when everyone else told her it was impossible. When I contemplated leaving my corporate job, I, too, had to find supportive voices to help me dismiss the deafening choir of well-meaning friends and family. "You can't change careers so late in your life!" I heard over and over. "Why don't you look for another corporate job in marketing and media?" or "You're crazy, this is far too risky, especially with two young kids!" Never mind that I had followed that professional path only to make a living, rather than out of genuine interest. Not to mention that I'd never felt at home in traditional corporate environments.

Luckily for me, every time I heard that changing career lanes just wasn't done so late in the game, I also had my friend Sandrine to remind myself this wasn't true for everyone. Several years earlier, Sandrine had seemingly been at the top of her game, having made partner at a major strategy consulting firm. Then she shocked her colleagues and some of her friends when, well into her 40s, she decided to take advantage of a generous corporate severance package to quit, go back to school, and become an architect. She'd always wanted to study architecture but had settled for business studies and a consulting career instead, deemed "safer." A few years later, with her degree in hand, she partnered with another woman to open a new architecture practice, which became very successful. If the *it's-too-late-to-change-career* collective voice, widely accepted as conventional "wisdom," wasn't true for her, why should it be true for me? All I needed was a transition plan and to know when to ask for help. Throughout that journey, I met new people, new voices that were closer to mine, and I ended up rebuilding my entire life from the ground up: newly single, with a new professional direction and new friends. My first successful career transition added fuel to my inner voice when, a few years later, I decided to use my experience to help others by becoming a coach. By then, no external voice, whether individual or collective, could have stopped me.

Is It Relevant?

But what if the voice is true for you? What if you genuinely agree? Then put the external voice that has been feeding your mindtrap to the test of an alternative question: Is it relevant?

David

Do you remember David, introduced in Chapter 2? David's mindtrap was inherited from his European parents and grandparents, who had survived World War II hiding and fearing that anyone, anywhere, could betray them at any moment. David grew up listening to their war stories at the dinner table, absorbing their perspective that the world was a dangerous place where no one could be trusted. At work, David was hiding behind the walls of his arcane technical knowledge, in which he kept drowning his colleagues and his team. Because no one completely under-stood what he was talking about, he made sure that his special-ized skills remained unmatched and unique, and that everyone knew it, which kept his position unchallenged and safe. As if this wasn't enough protection, he often went on the offensive with his peers and his team, none of whom he trusted, which created constant friction. Once his mindtrap traveled from his uncon-scious to the bright light of his awareness, David realized that he was behaving as if permanently under siege.

Was his parents' and grandparents' perspective true? It had certainly been true during the war, and their extreme vigilance and distrust had helped them survive. But was it relevant for David? Was there a war going on in his office? No. Was his envi-ronment dangerous? Not particularly. Would his life be in danger if he dismantled the walls of his invisible fortress? Absolutely not. What about his job and his position? Almost certainly not. His family's understandable perspective belonged to them and their story, but it wasn't relevant to David's situation.

How did you learn to ride a bike as a child? When I got my very first bike, it came with two training wheels, so I could learn to ride without falling. Maybe it was the same for you. But do we still ride our bikes with training wheels attached today? I don't know about you, but I don't. Why? Because once I knew how to keep my balance, the training wheels were no longer help-ful. What was once a support became extra weight. Some of the voices that still live in our heads are like these training wheels: extra weight we carry around that serves no purpose any longer and slows us down.

Let's go back to Claire. She had concluded that she wasn't messy after all. But what if she had been? Would it be so ter-rible? Claire realized that it wouldn't. Her house and her desk didn't have to be perfectly tidy all the time. Her mother's voice had been pulling Claire's strings, but she could now see that it was no longer relevant in her life.

Buddha

If you find yourself trapped in an endless parade of "I should" and "I must" and "I have to," then it is time to examine whether the voice behind your mindtrap is relevant. This is exactly what Siddhartha Gautama did—not once, but twice. Born into a wealthy and powerful family, he lived a sheltered, refined, and opulent existence, wanting for nothing and unaware of life outside of his mansion's walls. When he was 29 years old, however, he ventured outside. What he found shocked him. In quick succession, he saw an old man, a sick one, and a dead body. And for the first time, it dawned on him that this happens to all humans, regardless of how much money one might have. That suffering is part of human life was not good news for Siddhartha. Suddenly, he found the path he'd been on completely irrelevant to him. What was the point of a life of indulgence, wealth, and power if, ultimately, all this couldn't shield him and the people around him from suffering? He felt as if he'd woken up to a whole new reality, and his entire perspective changed—his first mindshift. He decided that he would spend his life trying to figure out how to end this suffering. But how?

On the way back to his palace, he saw a very skinny man meditating. Back then, according to conventional wisdom—or what I'd call a collective voice—the path to end human suffering was clear. it required taming our constantly dissatisfied mind and its pointless pursuit of external gratification, which, like drinking salty water when thirsty, brings only fleeting satisfaction rather than genuine contentment. And the only way to do that was to renounce all comfort—forget luxuries like food, sleep, and sex— and spend one's life meditating. So, Siddhartha left his life behind and became an ascetic, starving himself, sleeping on nails, and begging for his subsistence. He believed that was what he *should* do. He became skeletal. After six years, however, he found that all the deprivations hadn't done much for his enlightenment.

Instead of sticking to the collective voice—that the only path to spiritual growth was a life of extreme deprivation—he concluded that all this starving and sleeping on nails was just as irrelevant to finding the answers he was looking for as his old life of indulgence. He concluded that there must be another path, or a middle way, to find enlightenment and lasting happiness within by taming his mind, and he would find it. So he started eating again. All the other ascetics accused him of going back to his old ways. He lacked strength and commitment, they said. Siddhartha, however, held firm, ignoring the collective clamor that had become irrelevant to him and instead following his own inner voice. He sat under a fig tree and decided he wouldn't move until he'd figured it out. And this is where he found what he'd been looking for—nirvana—and became known as Buddha.

Don't worry, I'm not suggesting we all sit under a tree and become buddhas. But we all have some cleaning up to do in our minds, getting rid of external perspectives that we still carry like training wheels, even though they are no longer true or relevant to who we've become.

Mateo

Mateo is the successful senior executive whose happy childhood disintegrated after his father succumbed to addiction. Years later, Mateo kept racing forward, his eyes always on the next prize and never satisfied with himself, in part because he was saddled with guilt that he *should* have done more to save his father.

"Did your father ever ask you for help?" I said.

Mateo admitted his father never did.

"So why do you believe that you could have saved him? Or that it was up to you to save him?" I asked. "Are you God?" I then joked to lighten the seriousness of the questions.

Mateo was beginning to understand that, in the context of his father's demons, what he did and could have done was irrelevant.

Ultimately, the only demons we can successfully battle are our own. Deconstructing his guilt brick by brick made space for a new perspective.

Is It Still Helpful?

This brings us to our next critical question: Is the voice behind your mindtrap still helpful? In other words, does it benefit you more than it costs you?

Andrew

Andrew had no doubt that his professor's perspective was not at all helpful to him today. First, as previously argued, the world has changed, and the superhero, hard-nosed approach to leadership is no longer considered a model. More important, Andrew didn't identify with this vision of the unflappable and infallible leader unencumbered by emotions. He both wanted and felt that he needed to be a different kind of leader: more caring, more supportive, and less distant. When we worked together, the COVID-19 pandemic was sweeping through the world. His teams were worried about their own health and their loved ones', and about their jobs. Factories had to close, and lockdowns were in place, contributing to uncertainty and isolation. To Andrew, issuing directives from the mountaintop had never felt less appropriate or effective. Instead, he wanted to be in the trenches with his staff, reassuring them that, even though no one knew what the future held, together they could find a way forward.

Claire

Another, more indirect way to explore whether a perspective or mental construction is still helpful is to ask yourself the following: Does this give me joy or energy? If not, what you're doing is like pouring sugar in the tank of your car. Claire, for example, woke up very early every morning so she could swim for one hour before going to work.

"Do you enjoy swimming?" I asked her.

"I used to," she said. "But I'm often feeling so exhausted that I have to push myself to go, and then I feel even more tired when I come out of the pool."

Claire was spending so much time in the pool that swimming had gone from being a joy to something that sucked energy out of her. "So why do you swim so much?"

She had to think about it. "If I want to look after my health," she finally said, "I *should* exercise!"

That exercising contributes to good health was true enough. It was also relevant. But here it was, the "I should" that siphons out any joy that one might find in anything. Did she have to swim *every day* to be healthy? And for one hour? No! Was it healthier to be constantly exhausted or to take time to refuel her tank? So, the health argument wasn't helpful. What about pushing back a little, so she could reclaim some joy from swimming and actually draw some energy from it? Compare Claire with another executive who exercised one hour a day. For him, exercise was a way to avoid burnout, maintain balance, and stay calm. There was no "I should," but rather "I want." In his case, that amount of exercise was helpful.

What about the expectations of Claire's parents and their definition of success? To some extent, that "voice" had been helpful in the past. It had pushed her to develop skills that had served her well—she had, after all, been a brilliant student and put her business degree to good use. But continuing to set aside her emotional intelligence and intuition was not helpful. Claire now saw that these could be enormous strengths. As she embraced these qualities, she started noticing people around her who were like her. They didn't consider themselves isolated, weird, or inadequate. She came across books, articles, and conversations validating her new perspective that the traits she had been trying to suppress were in fact assets. She was ready to accept, integrate, and show all parts of herself with her colleagues and her team. She did not yet know how, however.

What if you believe the voice behind your mindtrap is helpful? Make sure that you've properly thought this through, and that you've considered the dark side of any quality or strength when pushed too far.

Now you're ready to consider what mindsets you'd like to keep, what you want to let go, and what you'd like to adopt going forward. In other words, which voices, feelings, and attitudes do you feel grateful for? Which no longer serve you, or never did, and weigh you down like a heavy backpack you've been slogging for years? And which new mindsets and attitudes could help you step into your authentic self? Think of it like going through old boxes in your garage.

Claire, for instance, was keen to let go of her parents' vision of success, which she didn't truly identify with, and her need for their approval. She was grateful for the perspective and skills she had developed through her business education and experience, which she would keep. And she wanted to adopt a new mindset about intuition and emotional intelligence. Similarly, David wasn't at war, so why would he hold on to a vision of the world as a dangerous, hostile place full of people who couldn't be trusted?

What about you? What would you write in each of your three columns—keep, let go, and adopt?

* * *

Is it true? Is it relevant? And is it still helpful?

These questions are meant to challenge our mental constructions, so we can first decide whether to keep them or not. Then we have a decision to make: Are we ready to let our mindtraps go? Because to shine our light in the world, sooner or later we need to live according to who we really are, and not who we think we should be.

SELF-REFLECTION

1. **Truth be told**
   - Examine the voice(s) behind the mindtrap you most want to tackle. What evidence debunks them? And what evidence do you have that they are true?
   - If your answer is "one should . . .," who said that? Can you identify who "one" is?

2. **Is it relevant?**
   - Is that voice still relevant?
   - Who are your role models? Why? Are they still relevant for you?

3. **Is it still helpful?**
   - Are the voice(s) behind your mindtrap still helpful?
   - Does the behavior associated with your mindset energize you or drain you?
   - Create three columns and answer these questions: What mindsets and associated behaviors do you want to drop, keep, and adopt? What actions can you take to move in that direction?

CHAPTER 7

Challenge Your Fears

Three Strategies to "Do It Anyway"

After meeting the goblin, the child realizes he does not need the foreign princess after all. Then an idea pops in the child's head: What if he goes to the edge of the forest? Perhaps the view is clearer from there. Perhaps the path of roses is even visible.

The child walks and walks, until he reaches the edge of the forest, which ends at a cliff. Beyond is a strange land he has not yet visited. A white-bearded magician stands on the other side. Right behind him, the child sees the beginning of a path framed by magnificent rose bushes.

"Come this way," says the magician, extending his hand with a smile.

"I'm scared!" says the child.

"What are you afraid of?"

"I've never been so far out! This forest is all I know. What if I get lost? And I don't know how to cross! There is no bridge to the other side."

"Of course, there is!" says the magician. "You just cannot see it yet. But I will help you."

The child looks at the cliff again. He can now see a small bridge that connects to the other side.

"Are you ready?" asks the magician.

Before the child can answer, a snake slithers by. The snake's name is Yezbutt.

"What are you doing?" the snake asks.

The child explains that he wants to cross to the other side to find the path of roses.

"Yes, but you don't have the right shoes! You cannot cross until you have the right shoes."

The child looks at his bare feet. Does he really need shoes? He looks at the magician, who is still smiling. "I walk barefoot all the time," the child replies.

"Yes, but the sun will set soon," Yezbutt then points out. "You shouldn't walk in the dark. Better wait until tomorrow morning."

The child looks at the sky and sees the moon has already risen. "The moon is full tonight," he says. "It will light my way."

Yezbutt hisses, but no word comes out. Perplexed, it slides away.

"Now I am ready," says the child.

* * *

Having challenged the voice that keeps your mindtrap alive through questions, you now have a decision to make. Are you ready to release it? Are you ready to leave behind the baggage that has been weighing you down?

You might be wondering why you need to answer this question at all. Why go through all this mindtrap business if not to move past it? But taking a moment to make this decision is a crucial step in the mindshift process. Consciously drawing a line in the sand opens our mind to what follows. It is a signal to our brain that we give ourselves permission to move forward. When we send that signal, we start noticing different things around us. We typically used to focus only on the people, events, and words that kept our mindtrap alive, but now we can see and hear around us what used to pass us by: people, events, and words that support our mindshift.

Having challenged our mental constructions does not mean that letting them go is always easy. Sometimes it is, and some mindtraps, once uncovered, drop like overripe fruit from a branch. But to successfully and durably shift our most challenging mindtraps, there are obstacles to be removed and objections to work through. First, change is intimidating, and the fears outlined previously—fear of your own emotions, fear of chaos, and fear of failure—are likely to rear their heads with a vengeance, keeping you in what you know. Our brain finds comfort in the familiar, and although change brings opportunities, it also carries risks and costs. No mindshift is possible until we acknowledge these fears and, as psychologist Susan Jeffers puts it, "feel the fear . . . and do it anyway."[1] How do we "do it anyway"? How do we feel our fear and still decide we can let go?

Think of your decision as a scale: on one side is the status quo and on the other is change. Our brain weighs each side according to one main measure: What can I gain from it? On the side of the status quo is some sense of safety associated with what's familiar, but also dissatisfaction and limitations. On the side of change is the cost of what we're letting go and the risk of the unknown, but also the potential of something better. When any or several of these ingredients change, so does the balance of the scale. The good news is, there are several things we can do to help us tilt the scale toward change:

- See the gift in crises.
- Organize support.
- Take one step at a time.

See the Gift in Crises

When asked recently about the worst moment of her career, British singer-songwriter Adele didn't have to think. On January 20, 2022, the day before she was scheduled to kick off a Las

Vegas residency, she announced in an emotional video posted on Instagram that she was canceling it. "My show ain't ready," she said. "I can't give you what I have right now." She'd been agonizing for a week, unable to decide what to do. She was terrified at the thought of letting everyone down: her team, who'd been working hard on the show for months in the midst of another COVID-19 surge; investors who'd put up vast amounts of money; and most of all, the fans who'd booked tickets, many of whom would not only be terribly disappointed but also lose the money they'd already spent to travel to Vegas.

So how was she able to put aside so much pressure and fear? How was she able to see clearly what the right decision was for her? The show hadn't felt right to her for a while, but she didn't quite know why. During a dress rehearsal the day before, during the very first song, she got so frustrated that she stopped, walked to the very front of the 15,700-square-foot stage, sat down, and pulled her microphone away. Then, with no amplification and no music, she sang to thousands of empty seats. In that moment, looking into the front rows, she knew. This was the intimacy, connection with the audience, and unpretentious authenticity that her show was missing and that she'd been craving. And for an artist who owes her stratospheric success not only to killer vocals but also hyper-vulnerable songs and performances, going ahead would have been an unacceptable lie to her fans. Although the reaction was brutal, Adele says that it was the right thing to do. "It actually made my confidence in myself grow," she explains, "because it was a very brave thing to do."[2]

Adele could have listened to the collective voice telling her to keep the show. She could have let her own fear convince her that it was too late to postpone, because too many people would be upset and the cost to her reputation would be too great. But ultimately, the cost of silencing her inner voice and going ahead with something that she knew was wrong became bigger than her fear. What feels right to her is to put her true self out there completely—in her music, lyrics, and stage presence—which is essential to why she and her music resonate with so many people around the world. This is who she is as an artist. And, amidst the whirlwind of putting together a gigantic show, it took a moment of crisis for her to remember it. Adele hasn't let more than 15 years of stardom and over 120 million albums sold worldwide cloud her inner voice and compass.

How do we get that kind of clarity? We often don't, until life throws us a curve ball that hits us in the face. Chapter 5 describes how crises can help reveal our mindtraps. But crises sometimes carry more than one gift: they can also give us the courage to change. This is the "gift" I received years ago, when I was going through a difficult time. I had completely lost touch with who I was, but because I had lost my self-confidence, too, I kept convincing myself that I had a picture-perfect life, with two wonderful children and a prestigious corporate job.

It had been months since I'd dreamed of my grandmother telling me to find the path of roses, but I was too scared to make the changes I truly needed. The "push" factor was not yet strong enough when measured against the risks and the cost of leaving my corporate career and my marriage, which seemed overwhelming. I had nightmares that I was wandering in the street without shoes, homeless. I feared that I could not succeed if fully myself: I had come to believe that I was not analytical or linear or *anything* enough.

After growing up in a loving but very traditional family, I still carried the weight of conventions, too, which added to my fears: getting divorced was not "done." A conversation with a friend made that weight apparent. "What am I going to do?" I asked her, after telling her that I was wilting in a relationship that allowed me no space to be myself. "Nothing," she said. "You chose to get married, so you stay." So I feared my parents and most of my friends wouldn't understand, let alone approve, which would leave me alone and isolated.

I was stuck and lost, unable to decide what to do. Perhaps I was the problem? So when I first went to see a coach, I was not seeking help to change. I was seeking help to make the status quo work better for me. Then he asked whether I was willing and able to invest the time and effort into reconnecting with myself, and my heart sank. It felt like another demand on time and energy I didn't have.

My body helped tilt the scale. Shortly thereafter, I developed a skin rash, and a doctor diagnosed me with a mild case of hepatitis A. It was as if I'd been given permission to hit the pause button and take time off to take a good look at my life. The next day, I woke up so exhausted that I was utterly unable to get out of bed. I lost 10 kilos within one week. For several months, I couldn't get out of bed, and all I did was sleep. My inability to move forward had escalated to a physical inability to move, period. I had hit the proverbial wall. My doctor couldn't understand why I was so sick and so exhausted for so long, and he asked me what was going on in my life. For the first time, I was able to acknowledge and verbalize the crushing extent to which I had lost myself. I was so ill and exhausted that he had to put me on extended sick leave, which, once I was feeling well enough, gave me time and space to work with the coach I'd seen once. I had kept telling myself not only to squeeze into a life that was fundamentally at odds with who I was but also to enjoy it. I had spent so much energy for so long fighting against myself that I was completely depleted. My own body was signaling in no uncertain terms what my conscious self had been too scared to accept: it was time to make a change.

The intensity of my illness opened my eyes to the true cost of staying on the same path: I was clearly at the very end of my tether, and to keep going could mean staying incapacitated, or even dying—figuratively, but possibly even literally. My survival instinct kicked in. I wanted to live, and change and uncertainty started to feel less risky and frightening than the alternative. With the help of my coach, I became aware that tinkering at the edges of my current life wasn't going to cut it. I needed to remember who I was and rethink what I wanted out of life.

This is the gift of crises: they tilt the "status quo versus change" scale, making it easier for us to decide to let go of what's holding us back. For me, the cost of doing nothing had suddenly hit the roof. Was I still afraid? I was terrified! I had no idea how I could pull this off. But the fear of leaving my financial and social comfort zone paled when compared to what would happen if I didn't. In short, my health crisis gave me some clarity and the courage to "do it anyway"—or at least to take one first step toward change.

The COVID-19 pandemic is the type of crisis that tilted the scale for many people, particularly leaders. Faced with an unprecedented health crisis—both mental and physical—repeated lockdowns, a severe economic downturn, and extreme uncertainty, many leaders realized that they had to become different kinds of leaders to get a chance to weather the storm successfully. Take Andrew, whose traumatic oral exam as a young student had led him to believe that, to be successful, leaders had to have all the answers and keep all emotions aside. He'd been tempted to become a far more human leader, in line with who he was. But he'd spent all his career behaving differently, and he didn't know how to change his habits, which scared him. What if he botched everything by trying something new? What if he failed? After all, the traditional approach had served him pretty well: he was heading the subsidiary of a large industrial group and was the youngest of his peers. He had been considered to become CEO of the entire group, even if he hadn't gotten the job in the end. There was a lot to lose by changing how he led.

But when the pandemic broke out, he quickly realized that he could no longer stay on the same path. Coming up with solutions from the top was no longer possible because he had no idea what to do. There was no playbook to fix that kind of crisis. Also, how could he set aside all emotions when his teams were anxious about their own health and their families', worried about their jobs, struggling with isolation, and, for those with young families, feeling the pressure of juggling workloads with home-schooling? The unprecedented crisis gave him the nudge to "face his fear and do it anyway."

Once he'd made the decision, he learned how to lead differently. He spent a lot more time at the company's production sites, which risked having to shut down, to be there for local employees and work with them to find the best way forward. He learned to say "I don't know" when he didn't have the answers. He learned to ask more questions and listen better. When looking for solutions to problems, he learned to talk last—and less. And he learned to communicate more with his heart. During lockdowns, for example, when many office staff members were battling isolation and anxiety, he helped maintain a sense of connection by sending to everyone in the company regular video messages in which he shared news but also offered support. He organized regular video calls with no work agenda just to catch up with his direct team, and at the start of every meeting or conversation, he took a few minutes to check in. He wasn't shy to share some of his own challenges, which created space for others to do the same. He launched support services for staff members who were struggling with mental health. While doing all this, he kept feeding a sense of confidence that, if everyone worked together, they would find solutions to the problems they were facing.

For Claire, who had worked so hard to model her parents' expectation of success that she'd lost sight of who she truly was, the crisis that helped tilt the scale was her father's illness and death. She'd looked at her father as a role model all her life and had been battling a conviction that her career didn't measure up to his. After her father was diagnosed with cancer, she was both devastated and angry that he refused to undergo treatment. She was also hurt that, even though he knew his time was limited, he didn't spend more time with his family and kept focusing on work, as he'd always done. She kept hoping for heart-to-heart conversations, perhaps even some self-reflection on his part, none of which ever came. Then after his passing, she discovered that his financial affairs were a mess—a mess she was left to deal with. Claire was incensed. But once she eventually managed to get over her anger, her father's illness and death gave her the clarity and courage to decide that she was ready to stop seeing him as a hero to emulate. Like in *The Wizard of Oz*, the curtain had been lifted, and instead of the superhero she'd been looking up to all her life, she saw a human being, flawed like all of us. This gave her the courage to carve her own unique path, rather than keep trying—and, of course, failing—to become who she thought she was expected to be.

Luckily for us, we don't face existential crises like major illnesses, a worldwide pandemic, or the death of a loved one all the time. So, short of events that force our hand, what can we do to make sure fear doesn't stop us from deciding to let go of our mindtrap for good?

Organize Support

Long ago, the story goes, people used to think that finding a perforated coin brought good luck. Think of it as another version of the four-leaf clover. There was once a poor man who had not been very successful in his work and in life. But one day, miracle of miracles, he found a perforated coin. "Now that I have that coin, I'm going to succeed and prosper!" he thought. He kept the coin in a little pouch in his pocket, and every morning, he made sure that he could feel it and that it was with him before leaving the house. His life indeed changed. He became more successful at work. The more successful he became, the more he prospered. And the more he prospered, the more confident and admired he became. One day, he decided to look at his perforated coin—something he hadn't done in a long time. So, he took the pouch out of his pocket and took the coin out. But what came out was a coin that was not perforated.

Panicked, he ran to his wife. "This isn't my coin!" he exclaimed. "What happened? Who took my coin?"

"Your coat was dusty, so I shook it off through the window," she explained. "I'd forgotten about your coin, so it fell on the street. I ran downstairs and looked for it, but it was gone. I thought you'd be upset, so I put a regular coin in your pouch and put it back in your pocket."

"When did this happen?" the man asked.

"Two years ago!" his wife replied with a smile.

All this time, he'd trusted that his good luck coin was with him, and this was enough to give him the confidence he'd needed to succeed. But all along, the power and ability to succeed had been in him, not in the coin.[3]

It takes courage to face our fear, but the more confident we are, the less afraid we become. How can we give our self-belief a shot in the arm? Like the man in the perforated coin story, we borrow that confidence from something or someone. Finding a helping hand is critical to build and sustain confidence when we're afraid. Who believes in you at times you might not believe in yourself? Who has your back? Who can help you navigate the change you need to make? Chapter 5 argues how the right people can help you identify and shift your mindtraps. The same is true for confidence. That helping hand can be a coach, a spouse, or a friend. It can be a role model who has successfully traveled that same path before you. It can be a tribe of like-minded people who can help you bridge the gap between who you are as a leader and who you want to be, and who can walk by your side as you step into the unknown.

For Nike's CEO John Donahoe and his wife, Eileen, leaning on each other, on their community of friends, and asking for help has given them the confidence they could raise four children, have a fulfilling family life, and both pursue meaningful and demanding careers. Early in their relationship, they'd decided that they would "have it all"—marriage, family, careers—even if they didn't know how they'd do it. One critical element has been to support each other as equal partners by keeping a "positive-sum" mindset—they refused to think in terms of work against family or his career versus hers. When they faced what seemed like trade-offs, asking for help from each other and from the people around them gave them the confidence and the creative solutions that had eluded them.

When John was a young consultant at strategy consulting firm Bain, for example, Eileen started a legal clerkship. She had to be at the office early every morning, so John had to take their young children to school. But John was traveling a lot for work, and he couldn't see how to make it work. So he told his boss he was quitting his job. "Donahoe, you idiot," his boss told him. "You don't need to quit; we'll find a way to make it work." John then started advising a local client, so he could keep his job and take his kids to school in the morning. Years later, when President Obama asked Eileen to become the next US ambassador to the UN Human Rights Council in Geneva, she initially thought it would be impossible. John was then CEO of eBay, and their two youngest kids were still in high school. But their children gave her the confidence it could be done by saying, "You should do it! We'll make it work." Also, they both credit their like-minded community of friends for giving them the courage to believe it was possible to balance complex home and work lives. They all shared their struggles, encouraged each other, and offered practical help when needed.[4]

Bradley Cooper's 2018 version of *A Star Is Born* illustrates the power of someone else's confidence in us when ours alone is not strong enough to overcome fear. Unknown singer Ally, who works as a waitress, meets rock country star Jackson Maine in the bar where she works and performs covers. She lacks the confidence to sing her own songs, because she's been told over and over that her nose is too big, and that she won't make it in the music industry. But in a parking lot later that evening, she shares with him some lyrics she's written. "Can I tell you a secret?" he tells her. "I think you might be a songwriter." Impressed by her talent, he invites her to his next concert, where he starts performing her song and asks her on stage to sing it with him. Terrified, Ally initially resists. "All you have to do is trust me," he tells her. His confidence in her talent gives her the courage to face her fear and launches her career.

Richard Williams and his then-wife Oracene were confident that their two daughters could become world-class professional tennis players. That bulletproof confidence helped Serena and Venus believe it, too, back when few people would bet that African American girls from Compton had a shot at that dream. Today, thanks to their unprecedented success, an entire generation of young African American girls believe it, too.

What author Napoleon Hill labeled a *mastermind alliance* can also provide a much-needed confidence boost not only through the exchange of ideas and experience but also practical support. This is why former Facebook COO Sheryl Sandberg started an online initiative supporting women to achieve their ambitions through "lean-in circles." These circles are in-person or online communities that meet regularly to support their members. At the heart of the initiative is the conviction that "leaning in is not a solo sport." Similar groups and communities exist at all levels and across a wide range of interests, from venture capital incubators to CEO get-togethers such as the Business Round-table in the United States.

Many school sports teams have their "boosters"—supporters who promote the team and/or make financial contributions. So, as you contemplate whether you're ready to embark on a change, find your own boosters. Think of people close and far who can inspire and support you as you do so. Even one person can be enough.

Take One Step at a Time

Tackling obstacles in increments feels less intimidating than going for a big bang. When I was finally well enough to be able to get out of bed, I went back to the coach I'd seen once several months earlier. It took me another year to be ready to make a change. My own mindshift, and the decision to act on it, did not come either fast or all at once. There were many "yes, buts" to go through. Where would I live? What would I do for a living? How would I make sure my kids' lives didn't get upended? I was not yet able to see what the future would look like. My coach and I worked through all my objections one by one, and a transition plan started taking shape in my mind.

"Is there anything else that keeps you?" my coach asked after several months of working through all the excuses and "yes, buts" that had been keeping me stuck. His support helped bolster my confidence that it was possible to make a change. So did breaking down the Change with a capital *C* into smaller, more palatable changes. I decided there and then that I was finally ready to let go. Had I figured everything out? No! But I had enough of a transition plan and confidence that I could make it work to decide I was ready.

In Joseph Campbell's parable of the baby tiger and the goats introduced in Chapter 3, the baby tiger is ready to let go of the idea that he's a goat only when a grown tiger insists that he belongs to the striped feline species and then gives him some gazelle meat to eat. But what would have happened if the baby tiger had tried to eat the entire gazelle in one go, after all he'd eaten for years was grass? He would probably have choked to death. He first ate one bite and felt how his change in diet gave him some strength he didn't know he had.

Change doesn't have to happen all at once, especially when it comes to big changes. We sometimes must break it down in smaller, more digestible chunks. Remember the wise words attributed to Theodore Roosevelt: "Each time we face our fears, we gain strength, courage, and confidence in the doing." We all learn to walk one step at a time by putting one foot in front of the other—not by trying to run a marathon from day one. The question is: Are you ready to take that first step?

This is something David, the top executive who saw the world and people around him as hostile and dangerous, needed reminding. Having lived all his life with the mindtrap that only family could be trusted and counted on, he'd cared for his sick and aging parents alone, because he was an only child. After his parents had passed away, he felt he'd neglected his own children in the process, which fed a renewed dose of guilt and self-imposed obligations. At the same time, unable to trust his team and peers at work, he'd not only been hypervigilant but also combative. Unsurprisingly, David was exhausted.

"What would happen if you no longer felt at war and no longer felt guilty?" I asked him.

As David imagined what life could be like if he let go, his face and his shoulders relaxed. It was as if an enormous weight was lifting. "I'd be happy," he said.

"Do you want to be happy?"

"Yes!" he immediately replied without thinking. Then his rational self caught up with his imagination, as he mentally surveyed the gap that needed to be bridged. "But I don't know how to do that!" he then added, visibly anxious.

"One step at a time," I said.

* * *

You have a decision to make: Are you now ready to let go of your mindtrap and the voice associated with it? Are you committed to adopting a new perspective and nurturing it so it grows solid roots in your mind?

If you are, then let's proceed to weeding out the unconscious roots of your mindtrap to make space for your new mindset.

SELF-REFLECTION

1. See the gift in crises

- Think of a crisis you've experienced. What did you learn from it? How did it shape you?
- Did you decide to make changes as a result? What silver lining can you see?

2. Organize support

- Who believes in you? Who supports you? Who and what gives you confidence in yourself? Whom do you trust?
- Do you have a mentor or a role model?
- Do you have a mastermind group or support circle?

3. Take one step at a time

- Think of a change you'd like to make. Can you break it down in smaller steps? What step comes first?

CHAPTER 8

Let It Go

Three Ways to Make Peace with the Past

Having dealt with Yezbutt the snake, the child is now determined to cross the ravine and join the magician on the other side. He has said out loud that he is ready. He takes a minute to look at the forest behind him to say goodbye. But when he tries to take a step toward the bridge, he struggles to move. Vines have grown around his feet. The harder he tries to lift his feet, the tighter they become.

He looks to the other side for help; he cannot see very clearly into the distance. The path of roses quickly vanishes into the clouds, and there is no telling where it leads. Even the magician appears slightly out of focus. Is he real, or is the child making him up?

"I have vines around my feet, and I cannot see where I'm going," the child says to the magician. "Are you still there?"

"I am always with you, even when you can't see me," says the magician. "Because we are one and the same person."

The child is perplexed. "What do you mean? I've never seen you before!"

"That's because you've never gazed at this side before, but I've been waiting for you. Many years ago, I was you. And I am who you can be in the future, once you have crossed to this side. I have had a long and wonderful life."

A long and wonderful life? The child feels better, and his feet feel lighter.

"Listen to my voice," says the magician. "It will guide you."

* * *

Now your rational self is ready to let go of the mindtrap that is keeping you from becoming an effective human leader. But this is not enough. Why? Because you cannot only *think* your way out of it. Letting go of an old perspective and replacing it with a new, more helpful one also requires accessing your unconscious and intuitive self.

Think of mindtraps as weeds. It's hard to grow anything in the garden of your mind if it's overgrown with weeds. Thanks to our mindshift, they're no longer visible above ground. But unless they've been properly rooted out from our unconscious and replaced with seeds for new plants, they'll choke these seeds and grow back quickly. Making sure your unconscious no longer carries the remnants of your mindtraps is the last step in your mindshift.

The remnants I'm talking about here are what renowned psychiatrist and author David Hawkins has described in his book *Power vs. Force*. He has mapped emotions on a spectrum based on whether they expand or drain our energy. At the lowest-energy end of the spectrum is shame. On the highest-energy end is enlightenment. Courage sits somewhere in the middle, separating the emotions that drain us of energy—like those often related to fear such as guilt, grief, anger, or pride, as well as fear itself—from the emotions that uplift us—think acceptance, love, joy, or being at peace.[1]

Mindtraps are associated with low-energy emotions. However, a sustainable and productive mindbuild, when we adopt and strengthen a new perspective that supports new behaviors, can only grow amidst high-energy emotions. So we must make sure that the low-energy emotions typically associated with our mindtraps have given way to high-energy ones. Otherwise, they will keep us tethered to the very thoughts and external voices that we've decided to shift out of our way, and as a result, block the profound transformation needed to become a genuine and authentic human leader.

How do we access our unconscious and intuitive self and make sure our old mindtraps are no longer taking emotional space? We cannot tap into that part of ourselves through rational thinking. We must communicate with it indirectly, through visualizations, stories, and metaphors. Psychiatrist and trauma expert Bessel van der Kolk, for example, has described how people who've suffered trauma can heal through drama and theater. The idea is to help them connect with feelings they've been trying to bury by having them step into another character who voices these feelings. In one program, a 59-year-old Vietnam veteran who'd been hospitalized for detox dozens of times was tasked with practicing a few lines from William Shakespeare's *Julius Caesar*. In these lines, Brutus remembers the Ides of March when Caesar was assassinated. The veteran initially mumbled the lines. The challenge was to have him connect with what the words evoked for him, so he could embody the emotions of a fictional character. With each word that Brutus speaks in the play, like *remember*, *justice*, or *stab*, the program coach whispered in the veteran's ear asking what it was like to remember, whether he'd ever stabbed someone or had been stabbed in the back, what justice meant to him, and so on. On the first day, the veteran ran out of the room. The next day, he managed to stay, sweating and his heart racing as he associated words and situations from the play with his own life. And by the end of the program, he had let go of his demons well enough to start his first job in seven years—a job he still held many months later.[2]

Psychiatrist Milton Erickson was a master at using stories and what he called teaching tales to access the unconscious and shift thought patterns. He firmly believed that we all have the inner unconscious resources to find our own solutions, even though we're not aware of it. His role, the way he saw it, was merely to create the conditions to help patients access these unconscious resources. He shared this principle through the story of a horse that wandered into his family yard when he was a young man.

He wanted to return the horse but didn't know whom it belonged to. So he mounted the horse, led it to the road, and let the animal decide which way to go. He intervened only whenever the horse veered off into a pasture to bring it back on the road. After a few miles, the horse walked into another man's yard. "How did you know this was my horse?" the man asked Erickson. Erickson said he didn't—only the horse knew. All he'd done was to keep it on the road and let it find its way home.[3]

There are multiple ways to cultivate your unconscious in a way that replaces the low-energy feelings associated with your mindtraps and the people behind them with love, respect, and gratitude. Following are three of my favorite exercises. Whenever you're ready, let's work through them:

- Let go of the rope.
- Rewrite your story.
- Travel through time.

Let Go of the Rope

Have you ever played tug-of-war? You hold one end of a rope, your opponent holds the other, and you both pull in opposite directions. As long as you both keep pulling, you can't move much, and the game continues—until someone lets go of the rope. The same goes with challenging feelings—they keep us stuck in place—so I like to use this tool with people whose mindtrap is connected to a specific person or several people. Don't worry, there are no actual ropes in my office: I'm talking about an imaginary game. When used properly, such a visualization helps create a healthy distance and rebalance relationships, which helps substitute emotions such as anger, grief, or guilt with acceptance, gratitude, and peace. The idea is not to settle scores, abandon or hurt anyone, and it isn't to resolve anything for anyone else or understand their behavior, either. The objective is to free ourselves from any voice, baggage, experience, or perspective that does not belong to us—and any challenging emotions associated with them—in a spirit of love, respect, and gratitude so they no longer burden and limit us. The goal of this exercise is to bring us closure and peace, so we can spread our wings, be more of ourselves, and follow our own path unencumbered.

Sit comfortably, close your eyes, and take a deep breath. Whenever you're ready, visualize yourself on one side of a river pulling on a rope. Across the river and pulling on the other side of that rope is the person or people related to the mindtrap you've decided to drop. It could be the person whose voice stands in your way. It could also be something or someone that represents the stereotype or social norm that keeps you stuck. Each one of you is pulling, so you're locked in a tug-of-war. Then, imagine yourself suddenly letting go of the rope. If guilt, shame, or grief leaves you worried that whoever's on the other side may get hurt falling backwards, let's add an imaginary sandpit or even a soft mattress behind them. Imagine everything that unfolds after you drop the rope. What happens to you? What happens to the other person? What do they do and say? What do you do and say? How do you feel? Then once every draining or heavy emotion is gone, imagine yourself walking away on your side of the river.

Walter

Walter, a top executive in the service industry, struggled to completely let go of his mindtrap, which had grown from his mother's social insecurities and her desire to fit in at all costs. His rational self was keen to break free from his eagerness to please, always say the right thing, and ruffle no feathers, because it left little room for spontaneity and for being himself. Also, he systematically overprepared for any meeting, which meant he'd suggest solutions before listening to anyone else's. He'd made it to CEO, so he no longer needed to work so hard to prove that he belonged. Although he felt his behavior had contributed to his success, his leadership position now required something else of him. He had to switch from "know-do" to "be" to inspire and give the tone to his teams. But on a deeper, unconscious level, changing his behavior meant betraying his mother, who he felt had sacrificed so much for him. When I suggested this exercise, he initially resisted because he didn't want to visualize her being destabilized and perhaps fall. In addition to suggesting he add lots of extra virtual padding behind the mental image of his mother, I appealed to his own parenting emotions to shift his perspective.

"Do you love your children?" I asked.

"Of course!" he said.

"What do you most wish for them, now and going forward?"

He thought for a few seconds. "I want them to be themselves and make their own choices. And I want them to be happy," he said.

"Imagine them all grown up. They're the same age you are now. Who gets to decide what makes them happy?"

"They do!"

"Do you think your mother wished anything different for you?" I continued.

Walter smiled. "Okay, I'm ready for the tug-of-war now."

Once he let go of the imaginary rope, he explained to his mother that it was time for him to follow his own path. He understood why it had been so important for her to be accepted, and fitting in his new environment had helped him when he was a child. But it was now more important that he be true to his own voice. He thanked her for all that she'd done for him and told her how much he loved her. I asked him to imagine what his mother looked like and what she said.

"She looked surprised at first, but now she's smiling," he said. "She's telling me how proud she is of who I've become." The exercise helped Walter let go of the lingering guilt that kept him tethered to a mindtrap he wanted to shift.

Andrew

The visual tug-of-war works to remove other kinds of lingering feelings, too, such as anger, sadness, or fear, so we can prepare a healthy ground for our mindbuild. Andrew, the senior executive who embraced a new leadership approach during the COVID-19 pandemic, imagined a tug-of-war with his father. As a child, Andrew used to be afraid of him because his father never missed an opportunity to twist good things into bad and belittle people around him. Tired of being compared to a one-eyed king in the land of the blind, Andrew had even stopped making any effort at school at some point—until he'd realized that he was shooting himself in the foot far more than he riled his father. During our exercise, when Andrew dropped his end of the rope, his father fell and exploded in a torrent of complaints and insults.

"What are you feeling?" I asked Andrew. After our work together, Andrew had already gone a long way toward silencing his father's voice and shifting the associated mindtrap. But I wondered whether some challenging emotions might remain.

Andrew took his time to answer. "Nothing," he said. "Seen from here, he actually looks a little silly gesticulating and shouting like that." Andrew's lack of fear, sadness, anger, or other challenging emotions signaled that he was genuinely at peace with his father, who no longer was the giant of his childhood. His unconscious had absorbed that he wasn't responsible for his father's behavior and attitude, which no longer held any power and influence over Andrew's mindset, feelings, or behavior.

"Are you okay with continuing your journey?" I asked him.

"Yes," he said without hesitation. He then visualized walking forward along the river, free to move at his own pace, his father's angry voice growing fainter and fainter as distance grew, until it could no longer be heard at all. "I'm feeling much lighter!" he then exclaimed with a smile. The roots of Andrew's mindtrap had been pulled out from his unconscious, leaving space to plant something new.

Depending on our own preference and the nature of our mindshift, we can also bypass our rational self and access our unconscious through other means. Besides the tug-of-war visualization, I use tools to help rewrite our stories, which help solidify our mindshift and prepare our mindbuild.

Rewrite Your Story

Imagining events in your life unfolding in a positive way is a particularly effective tool to substitute challenging feelings related to your mindtrap with more positive ones. To put this into practice, let's go to "the movies." This is a particular kind of show, however. First, you're not going to the movies literally but, you guessed it, in your mind. Second, you're wearing multiple hats: not only will you be watching the movie from your seat in your imaginary theater but you'll also be the main character, the director, and the screenwriter. The idea is to step out of yourself and take a step back. Being both on the screen and in the theater allows you to imagine any situation and conversation from a distance, as if it is happening to someone else, which makes everything possible and gives you a different perspective.

This tool is particularly effective when dealing with unresolved grief or loss. Take Frank, whose restlessness and busyness hid the guilt and sadness he felt over the death of his friend and business partner. We agreed the objective of the exercise would be for him to tell his friend what he'd never had a chance to tell him before he died, so he could let go of the emotions that kept him from moving forward. His visual movie took him to a beach in California, where he as the main character was walking one evening after work to go have a drink with his friend, as they used to do. He met his friend at a beach bar, where they settled at a table looking out on the sea and ordered a glass of wine. They broke into a familiar banter.

"What does the main character tell his friend?" I then asked.

"I miss you," Frank said after a while. "You've helped me so much with the business, and I've never had a chance to thank you enough. So thank you! You've been a great friend, and I wish I'd helped you more. So what can I do for you now?"

"And what does his friend say?" I continued.

"Just take care of yourself, be happy, and move on with your life."

By the end of the exercise, I could see that Frank was at peace. Visualizing and telling his friend what he'd never had a chance to say had helped him alleviate the guilt and grief he'd been trapped into. He'd told him what had been weighing on his mind, and his friend gave him "permission" to move forward. It was time to end the visualization and come back to the present. He was free to remember his friend with joy and focus on honoring his life.

Now, it's your turn. Start by sitting comfortably somewhere silent and close your eyes. Select which person or people at the root of your mindtrap you want to include in the cast. These are people related to these challenging feelings we've been talking about. Choose a title and the set for your movie. Ready? Now imagine you're walking on the plush carpet of a movie theater, heading toward your own private screening. As you push the door, visualize the dark screening room, with its rows of empty seats and its big screen. No one is there. Choose a seat and settle in. Feel the arm rests supporting your elbows, the soft cushion at your back. Perhaps you've brought some popcorn? A soda? Whenever you're ready, start the projection. Watch the title appear on the screen.

Visualize the setting you've chosen. Where does your story take place? What does it look and sound like? The main character appears. It's you, so you watch yourself on the screen from your seat. Perhaps your name is the same, or perhaps your character is called something different. It's up to you. What is the protagonist wearing? What is he or she doing? What does he or she feel? Early in the movie, the protagonist—you—is going to meet the character who still triggers some unresolved feelings. What are they doing? What do you as the protagonist want to say? And what does the other character say in response? How does the scene end?

This type of tool can be adjusted if writing works better than visualizing for you. If grief or anger, for example, still ties you to someone else, consider writing them a letter, telling them everything that has been left unsaid. Remember, as said previously, that the objective is not to settle scores or get answers but to free yourself from burdens that are not yours to carry. Don't overthink it, just let your hand move or your fingers type. The letter that Claire wrote her father after he'd died, for example, helped her let go of the anger and hurt she felt that he hadn't prioritized his health and his family over his work, and that he'd left her a financial mess to deal with. Alternatively, you could write down a dialogue, instead of visualizing a movie. Externalizing your emotions by giving them voice helps to let them go. To create even more distance, you can burn your writing or leave it somewhere meaningful to you.

What can you do if the draining emotions that keep you tied to your mindtrap are not specifically related to someone else, however? Then you can travel in time.

Travel Through Time

Whenever we confront challenging situations, fear and anxiety are natural responses, and old and familiar mindtraps might sniff the opening and attempt to sprout again. Will we be able to go over the hump? Will we succeed? Do we have the expertise? Surely everyone will realize soon that we're imposters who don't belong in positions of leadership. What if everything falls apart? What if we fail? Our stomach contracts, and our mind narrows. Traveling far enough into the future to calm and peaceful waters, past the storm of a crisis or the fog of uncertainty, helps snap us out of a contracted and energy-draining state. It helps inject confidence that we're able to survive and thrive, even if we don't yet see the path forward. The idea is to substitute fear and anxiety, which snuff out any creativity, with positive emotions such as calm, confidence, and gratitude, which can open the door to new ideas.

Ray, introduced in Chapter 2, was the CEO who was being pushed into retiring, which made him angry and anxious. First, we paused to look back at all that he had accomplished over his career. That made him realize that he had a lot to be proud of, and that he'd already accomplished what was important to him and made a real difference in the lives of others. Then, he went to the movies of his mind to confront the people who were forcing him to go, and as he kept going, I could see his anger gradually receding. His tone of voice and his words were becoming less harsh. His face and his shoulders were more relaxed, and his breathing slower. It was then time to work on his anxiety over what he would tell people when he left, because he hadn't yet figured out what he would do next. By then, he hadn't left his job yet, but his departure had been publicly announced. So, we prepared his travel into the future to the day of his farewell party. When working on his mindshift, he had decided the things from the situation he was leaving that he wanted to keep, drop, and gain: he felt he still had a lot to contribute and wanted to keep helping others; he would gain more time to spend with his family and more time to write, which was something he wanted to pursue. But he could feel that there were still unresolved feelings that prevented him from moving on from his job with no regret and looking forward to the possibilities that a new chapter offered him. So we agreed that the objective of his time travel would be to let that go so he could move on with a light heart.

I asked him to travel to the day of his farewell party and imagine the best possible version of it. He started by visualizing where it was taking place and the many colleagues he appreciated who were there to celebrate him and wish him well on his forward journey. So there he was, raising a glass surrounded by well-wishers. How was he feeling in that situation? Ray felt grateful and emotional, too, feeling the warm embrace of esteem and appreciation from all the people with whom he'd worked well over the years. He was also excited about the new adventure that was about to start for him and about the sense of possibilities it gave him. Then as his mind kept imagining that he moved from one person to the next during the party, he had a chat with his replacement as CEO, who asked him how he was and what he would be doing next.

"I'm doing well," he told him. "This gives me an opportunity to start a new chapter. I'm considering several exciting projects, but I can't talk about them yet." He then wished his successor all the best for his new job. At the end of the party, he was content and had gained a sense of closure. He was ready to move on.

"Now take a look from that moment back to the you sitting here with me," I said. "What do you want to tell him?"

Ray smiled. "You're free!" he said with a smile. The exercise helped him shift the draining and constricting emotions associated with his old mindtrap to make space for far more expansive ones that would sustain his mindbuild of figuring out how he wanted the next chapter of his life to unfold.

I, too, have turned to time travel whenever I felt an old mindtrap trying to worm its way back into my head. Years ago, top leadership coach Marshall Goldsmith invited me to join a select group of coaches, top corporate executives, business thinkers, and other leaders in their fields. Inspired by the teachers and thinkers who'd helped him, he'd assembled the group to generously share what he'd learned over the years, expecting that, in time, we'd do the same so we could leverage our collective impact. Our shared purpose? Make good leaders, whatever their field, even better. I felt honored to be chosen to join. I thought I would learn a lot and loved being part of the idea of paying it forward. But before traveling from France to New York City to attend the first meeting, old limiting thoughts and emotions reared their heads. Did I really deserve to be part of that group? Everyone looked far more accomplished than I felt I was. What if my English, which I hadn't spoken much in a while, wasn't good enough? Was I going to be scorned or criticized? Or perhaps ignored? By then, I was familiar with my own mindtrap so

I could recognize it, gently shift it out of the way with the battery of questions presented previously in this book, and also connect with my unconscious to replace the paralyzing fear it triggered with confidence and excitement.

So I traveled forward in time. I visualized going to the airport in Paris and being on the plane. I imagined arriving at the airport in New York and heading to my hotel. What would the room look like? What would I have for dinner? I imagined how comfortable and peaceful I would feel during the next day's meeting with the mastermind group. I saw myself flying back to Paris, elated with the positive experience, and looking forward to our group's next meeting. And it was that Hortense of the future who then looked back at the present-day Hortense and reassured her there was nothing to worry about. Thanks to that exercise, I was able to head to New York City with confidence and my mind at peace, ready for this new adventure.

What if things don't turn out well, though? After all, you might be thinking, not every situation has a happy ending. A variant of the time travel exercise is to travel in the future along two different paths: one where the current challenge you're facing is resolved positively, and the other, the worst-case scenario. Go through the catastrophic scenario step-by-step and imagine at each step what you do next. Go far enough into the future until you realize that you can survive crises and adjust to new situations, and that there is hope. From that place of hindsight, what would you say to today's you? If you prefer, you can also write down this dialogue with yourself. As always, the objective is to create some distance with whatever immediate challenge we're facing and realize that, regardless of the short-term outcome, we have the inner resources to rebound and thrive again.

* * *

This communication with our unconscious to weed out anything that might keep us tethered to old mindtraps and make space for new perspectives is best thought of as a process, not a one-off exercise. These are tools to keep with you, accessible any time you may need them. Any good gardener doesn't weed out their path of roses once, but regularly. Think about how long you might have held the perspective you've worked on shifting. This is how long your neural pathways have developed, strengthened with every thought or event confirming your perspective. It takes time to weaken these pathways so others can be built. The stronger the energy-sapping emotions have been connected to our mindtrap, the more work and perhaps time it takes to replace them. I typically take my clients through not one but several of these exercises, and not just once but several times. I still use these tools for myself. With time, they work faster.

Sometimes, we also weed out in phases, like peeling the layers of an onion. The first time I worked with entrepreneur Blake, who was running a successful business offering workspace solutions, much of our focus was on how his mindtrap manifested in his relationship with his business partner. Because Blake felt he didn't possess the qualities he associated with successful business leaders, he initially felt he couldn't be successful as an entrepreneur by himself and systematically deferred to his partner's opinion. As he realized their respective visions for the business were incompatible, he eventually decided that it was time to part ways and lead the company alone, according to his own vision. Blake was now free to continue walking along his path of roses by himself. Then three years later, he got in touch again, as he felt he needed to deepen the progress he'd made. His confidence and leadership had greatly improved, but his old insecurities had occasionally led him to fall into old traps. For instance, he sometimes let potential recruits' shiny résumés and prestigious academic pedigree influence his hiring decisions, even though their values and personality didn't fit his and his team's. So we went through some of these exercises again.

Now that we've learned how to clear weeds from our path of roses, what will we plant in it? What new perspectives and behavior do we want to grow in the space we've freed for our mindbuild?

SELF-REFLECTION

Little check-up

- Connect with the emotions associated with what you'd like to change and define them: Are you feeling regret, fear, shame, guilt, anger, envy, sadness, or perhaps hurt?
- Write down in one sentence or one title that speaks to you the objective of the exercises: substituting the emotions you've just defined with a sense of peace and closure.

1. Let go

- Close your eyes. Think of the tug-of-war exercise. Who (or what) is at the end of the rope?
- Pull on the rope. What happens?
- Are you ready to let go? If so, let go. What happens now? How do you feel? Describe what happens as you visualize walking away and moving forward.

2. Rewrite your story

- Go to your mind movie with your title in mind or write a story about the people or things that relate to your unresolved emotions.
- Where is the story taking place?
- Who's there? What happens? What do you see, hear, and say? What do you feel?
- How does the movie end?

3. Travel through time

- Think of an event in the future that makes you nervous.
- Time travel to that event. Who is there? What is happening? Imagine different scenarios. See yourself and how you react.
- End the event or keep traveling in time until you reach a positive outcome.
- Come back to the present moment. What does your future self say to today's you?

Repeat any or all these exercises every day until you feel your challenging emotions shift.

PART 3

Mindbuild: Lead
with Empathy

Becoming a human leader is a journey, not a destination. Part 1 was about understanding what a mindtrap is and identifying your own, as well as the voices behind it. In Part 2, you learned to shift your mindtrap out of the way. Now in Part 3, you need to adopt and maintain a new perspective and put your human leadership in practice—what I call *mindbuild*.

Think of mindbuild as your own unique path of roses. You've now found the beginning of it. But how would you like your path to look? What kind of roses would you like to plant? Which color and scent? And how many? It's up to each of us to create our own. Rose bushes also need to be carefully looked after to thrive. We need to care for them according to the seasons: sometimes we plant, sometimes we feed the seeds, sometimes we observe and protect the developing buds, sometimes we prune, sometimes we admire the roses' beauty and enjoy their scent, and sometimes we prepare for the new season, based on what we've observed and learned during the last one. We keep moving and changing, as life itself.

CHAPTER 9

Define Your Identity as a Human Leader

Two Ways to Build a Truer Version of Yourself

As the child listens to the magician's voice—the voice of his future self—the fog starts clearing. The child sees all the details on the magician's face now: the warmth in his eyes and the smile on his face. Feeling the peace in the magician's heart, the child's own heart grows bigger and stronger. The sun now shines on the path of roses, which are bright red and yellow. A light breeze blows, and the child can smell each flower. What a magnificent spectacle! Then the magician's face becomes smoother, and his white hair darkens. His face grows younger, until the child sees an exact image of himself, calling out to him. The moment he stops struggling against the vines around his feet, they fall off. Light as a feather and with the gentle spring breeze at his back, the child floats forward, keeping his gaze on what awaits him on the other side.

* * *

Let's take a few seconds to look at the road you've just traveled. You've identified what mindtrap has been holding you back and standing in your way of becoming a more human leader and where it comes from. You've shifted it out of the way, first by understanding that mindtraps are only stories our brain created and then by taking a look at yourself from a different perspective. You then challenged your mindtrap through a series of simple but critical questions: Is it true, relevant, or helpful today? You've also decided to let go despite some fear. And finally, you've done some spring cleaning in your unconscious to shift any lingering unhelpful emotions that might keep your mindtrap alive.

Because you've resisted the temptation to speed through the mindshift (or perhaps even skip it?), you've established a solid foundation for your mindbuild. Becoming a human leader requires a genuine and lasting inner transformation so we can show up as a fuller, truer version of ourselves. And it is that fuller, truer self who becomes the source from which we are then able to lead differently. Shortcuts, tempting as they typically are, are like building a house on sand or trying to upgrade the software on your computer or phone without upgrading the operating system: it's not going to work for long, if at all.

Now, what about this mindbuild business? We start with two steps:

- Understand what drives us—in other words, what is most important to us, what fundamentally motivates us, or what author Simon Sinek calls our "why."
- Envision who we want to be—particularly, but not exclusively, what kind of human leader we want to be.

How do we do this? We flex our imagination. And flexing our imagination happens to bring extra benefits that also make us better and more effective human leaders.

Understand What Drives You

From a young age, Ralph Lauren had a very unique sense of dress style, inspired by the old Hollywood movies he so liked to watch. As a teenager, he would assemble pieces he'd found in thrift stores or army surplus outlets in unexpected ways. Later, when he could not find what he wanted in stores, he asked a local tailor to make them for him. With no training in design—and in an era when designers made clothes only for women, not men—he decided to expand beyond his own wardrobe. A young tie sales rep, he started with what he knew: ties. Typical men's clothing was conservative back then, with ties narrow and plain. Ralph Lauren wanted his wide and interesting. After he had a tailor make a few ties the way he wanted, his wife, Ricky, and in-laws sewed the Polo label he'd just created at the back, and he went to

Bloomingdale's, the famous New York City department store, to offer them for sale. He was told they needed to be narrow, and his own label had to go. Ralph Lauren, who back then had very little money, flatly refused, packed up his ties and left.

Why did he walk away, and what gave him the courage to do it? An unshakable and crystal-clear sense of purpose did. His vision was so strong that Ricky fully backed and trusted his decision, even though she was nervous. Because for Ralph Lauren, ties—and later clothes and home furnishing—were, and still are, manifestations of a much broader aspiration for a world and lifestyle born in his mind, which epitomize his own version of the American dream. What drives Ralph Lauren has never been selling ties, clothes, or sofas, or becoming a famous designer. It is to invite everyone to join his dream of the quintessential American life.

Why is understanding our personal *why* such a fundamental building block to becoming an effective human leader? In other words, why invest some of your precious time in clarifying what drives you? First, because it acts as both a compass and an engine, guiding you and pulling you forward. And second, because to be effective, human leaders must be able to inspire that same pull in others. And that ability can only spring as an extension of their own *why*.

How does a strong sense of personal purpose act as our compass and our engine? Keeping sight of what is important to us and why we do what we do is our most reliable guide when we face tough choices and decisions, as Ralph Lauren's story illustrates. How do we chart a way forward in unprecedented situations, complex challenges, and extreme uncertainty—today's world? When there is no playbook and limited information, our only guide is purpose. It gives us a clear sense of direction.

A strong sense of purpose was indeed what guided Gail Miller after her husband Larry died in 2009. Now the sole owner of a business empire that included a chain of car dealerships, movie theaters, an NBA basketball team, and a sports arena, she faced a choice: she could sell the family business and live a cushy life ever after; she could keep the company and let her oldest son, who had become CEO when his father was sick, make all the decisions; or she could get actively and directly involved. To her, most important of all was to preserve the vision and values of a company that her husband has given his life to build so it could continue to enrich the lives of employees and of the local community the way it had for many years. She'd never held a job in the business, but she'd been fully engaged through her husband for decades. Because she'd been there since the company was created, she felt she was best positioned to secure the company's future and preserve its values. In fact, she felt she had to. Her sense of purpose made the decision easy—even though putting it in practice wasn't. Reserved by nature, she had to step into the limelight in what was largely a men's world of automotive, sports, and entertainment. She had to convince everyone that she was up to the task. Her decision to create a board of directors to plan for the company's future went against the grain. She had to accept that, in doing what she felt was right, she might not please everybody. But the clarity and strength of her purpose gave her the fortitude and the perseverance she needed. What surprised her the most throughout this journey? That from being invisible, she became a role model for women.[1]

In addition to being a compass, a sense of personal purpose is also our engine: by telling us why we do what we do, it motivates, energizes, and propels us through hard times, fear, boredom, or any challenging circumstances and emotions when it is so easy to get derailed. It keeps us on track.

This is something Bronnie Ware knows a lot about. In the early 1990s, she left a banking career in her native Australia, first to work in a bar on a tropical island and later in England, then in palliative care. During these years tending to the dying, people shared their regrets with her as they faced the end of their lives.

And she noticed that most people—men or women, regardless of their walk of life—kept expressing the same five common regrets:

- I wish I'd had the courage to live a life true to myself, not the life others expected of me.
- I wish I hadn't worked so hard.
- I wish I'd had the courage to express my feelings.
- I wish I'd stayed in touch with my friends.
- I wish I'd let myself be happier.[2]

Research has confirmed that, when looking back at their lives, most people regret what they didn't do far more than what they *did* do. And within the things they didn't do, their biggest regrets are not so much about unfulfilled duties and obligations, but rather about not living up to their ideal selves.[3]

From Personal to Collective Purpose

In addition to guiding you and keeping you on track, being clear about what drives you is a prerequisite for creating an environment in which others are inspired and able to do the same. In other words, it is an essential component of being an effective human leader. Why? Because the best way to unleash other people's potential and energy is to understand what drives each of them and channel it toward a common vision. What has been driving Ralph Lauren the man all these years, for instance, is directly reflected in his company's stated purpose "to inspire the dream of a better life through authenticity and timeless style." That collective dream, in turn, has inspired countless other people, from employees to customers.

Of course, a personal *why*, by itself, does not a successful business or an effective human leader make; it also takes a lot of hard work, skills, and persistence to get there. But ultimately, it is the strength and clarity of Ralph Lauren's own personal *why* that has underpinned the company's success for over 50 years— starting with a callback from Bloomingdale's, which decided to buy his ties after all.[4] Only leaders who are clear about what drives them and are able to connect that personal sense of purpose with their companies' can help their teams do the same.

So what drives you? What are the most important things to you? What do you want to accomplish in your life? How do you want to be remembered? Perhaps you already have crystal-clear answers to these questions, in which case, your mindbuild is off to a solid start. But, even if you do, the rest of this section gives you a chance to check in with yourself so you can confirm, refine, or adjust your outlook. It might also give you a fresh perspective that will surprise you.

What if we don't have clear answers? How can we better understand what drives us? Sudden and unexpected crises often give us a clearer sense of what's important to us in life. During the COVID-19 pandemic and its multiple lockdowns, for example, many people reexamined their priorities and decided to change how they live. Similarly, people who confront life-threatening situations typically gain a heightened sense of purpose. Take physicist Stephen Hawking, for example, who was in his early 20s when he was diagnosed with motor neuron disease and given only two years to live. Hawking himself said that, until that point, he had been an average student as a child and studied very little while at Oxford. But his death sentence gave him a sense of urgency to find his own voice. "When you are faced with the possibility of an early death," he wrote, "it makes you realize that there are lots of things you want to do before your life is over."[5]

Thankfully, we don't constantly face global pandemics or life-threatening illnesses. Short of these crises, how can we get that kind of perspective?

We flex our imagination and rely on our unconscious.

There are multiple ways to help us do this. In "The Heart of Business," for example, former Best Buy CEO Hubert Joly explains how he gained clarity on his own purpose from the spiritual exercises of Ignatius de Loyola.[6] For former Medtronic CEO Bill George, crucibles—the challenges that shape us—are key to defining and understanding what drives us, what he refers to as our True North.[7]

I use a variety of tools to help my clients connect with their own *why*, some of which I go into details in another book.[8]

But there is one exercise that I find particularly effective: writing your eulogy.

Write Your Eulogy

Do you remember the exercise introduced in Chapter 6 through Claire's story? To win her parents', and particularly her father's, approval, Claire had repressed whole parts of herself and followed a career path in line with their vision of success. Her homework after one of our sessions was to write her own eulogy—specifically how she wanted her family, her friends, and her colleagues to remember her. In that context, the exercise was to help her realize what her mindtrap had obscured: that she'd been chasing an ideal of success and of a life well lived that belonged to her parents, and particularly her father, which was in fact fundamentally different from hers.

That same exercise is strikingly helpful for zooming in on what's truly important to us through the noise of our conscious mind. Whenever we ask ourselves what fundamentally drives us, it is often difficult to see the forest from the trees. Without even realizing it, we're caught in our current circumstances, which drastically narrow our sense of perspective and our imagination. Projecting ourselves far enough into the future and looking back at our lives from that viewpoint does two things: it gives us enough distance and detachment from our current self and circumstances, which gives our imagination far more space to roam free; and watching in the rearview mirror from the end of the journey—or close to the end—also brings into perspective the kind of person we truly want to be and the impact we want to have.

So write your eulogy. What would you like it to say? What do you want your spouse, partner, siblings, and children—if you have any or imagine having any by then—to say? What about your friends and your community? And the people you worked with—your peers, your team, your boss, your board? The purpose of this exercise is meant to stretch your imagination forward and give you the benefit of perspective. The idea is also to look at all aspects of your life—not just your professional life—because we are whole individuals, not perfectly compartmentalized beings like in *Severance*, the TV show in which characters have their memories surgically divided between their work and home lives. But if the thought of your eulogy fills you with a sense of dread, then imagine your future self at a ripe old age instead. You're watching a documentary or reading a biography that has just come out about your life. What would you like the people around you to say about you when interviewed? Make sure you still cover family, friends, and colleagues. How do you feel about it? What is the older you saying about your own life and what are you most proud of? What emotions go through you when you are saying it?

Now come back to the present. Take time to write down your experience—a sentence or a paragraph to keep the essential. Or if you find this too difficult, even just a word that sums up the most important. Take time to digest. Writing my own eulogy helped me understand what fundamentally drives and motivates me: to listen to other people and help them see light, hope, and potential in themselves, in their own story and journey, and in others. I want to be remembered as someone who made a difference in people's lives by believing in them and helping them uncover and liberate who they truly are. Understanding and articulating what drives me is the reason I became a coach: it feels more directly aligned with that *why* than being an entrepreneur.

How do your ideal future self's qualities, behavior, and achievements align with who you are and what you're doing today? If they don't align, what changes do you want to make? By having you look at your life from that viewpoint, this exercise shines a light on what really matters to you and what drives you—in short, on your *why*.

It's now time to move to another foundation of your mind-build: a more detailed vision of your future self.

Imagine Your Future Self

Now we're creating a vision of what the fuller, bigger version of yourself in general—and as a human leader in particular—looks, sounds, and feels like. Why? Because what we first imagine, we can be. As a wise man said, "I become what I see in myself. All that thought suggests to me, I can do, all that thought reveals in me, I can become."[9]

Back to the Future

Visualize your future self. We are time traveling again, but for a different reason: the point of the exercise is to flex your imagination muscle to the fullest, unconstrained by today's circumstances and obstacles, so you create a vision of yourself that acts as a magnet and pulls you to become that version of you.

First decide which parts of your life you'd like to focus on. If you could wave a magic wand and anything was possible, what would you change? Transport yourself into the future so you can see, hear, and feel what it is like. What are you doing? Who are you with? What do you look like? Where are you and where do you work? You can also imagine specific situations. What are you saying and how are you behaving? How do you feel through these situations? Visualize it or write it down in detail. Notice any word, image, or behavior that resonates with you: these are critical clues of the self you want to unleash and the direction you want to go, and who you are as a human leader.

For example, Blake, the entrepreneur who'd been deferring to his older business partner because he didn't trust his own ideas, imagined himself 10 years ahead in his 40s. He imagined being retired, living in the countryside he loved so much. This gave him a deep sense of belonging, of being and doing exactly what he was supposed to. He visualized being someone whom other people came to for advice. He would welcome visitors, listen to them, and help in any way he could. This signaled to him that his vision of leadership was about listening to people to understand what they needed and wanted, and about supporting them in getting it.

This was in fact directly connected to the business he'd created. His company designed bespoke working spaces that were highly functional based on each company's specific needs, but also where people would feel comfortable, inspired, and energized. One of his strengths was his ability to connect with his clients and their employees on a very human level, so he understood what they needed and wanted, even if they were not able to articulate it clearly. His vision also aligned directly with the way he interacted with his own staff members, with whom he was keen to develop and maintain an equally deep connection so he could support and guide them.

Blake's visualization helped him clarify the kind of leader he wanted to be, which in fact had little to do with university degrees and the pedigree that he felt he lacked to be successful. It motivated him to become even better at listening and leveraging his intuition and empathy to clearly understand what others needed. And it also helped him trust that his perspective, ideas, and opinions were valuable. In short, he gave himself permission to manifest who he truly was and the kind of leader he wanted to be, which was liberating.

This exercise is particularly helpful when you feel stuck, unable to see past your current circumstances. During the worst of the COVID-19 pandemic, one of my CEO clients felt drained and exhausted, like many leaders during that period. Lockdowns meant stores had to close, employees had to work remotely, and others had to be furloughed. What was the best way forward? How could he fight multiple fires? How could he best support people who were anxious and burned out, without burning out himself? With no end in sight, he often felt lonely and overwhelmed. He wasn't sure he wanted to stay on as CEO going forward.

I asked him to imagine himself in 10 years. What was he doing? Who was there? What brought him joy? He visualized being home with his wife and children. They were playing football in the garden, laughing. He saw himself having dinner with friends, having a good time. He visualized having time to relax, reading, playing the piano, and going for a run. He had the space and freedom to go on holidays and recharge, without having to look at his phone. I then asked him to write it all down. As his brain experienced the life he wanted as if in the present, he was able to recharge. It also helped him skip past his challenges, giving him hope. Finally, it reminded him that he was free to make choices for himself: if he no longer wanted to be CEO in the future, he could opt for another path; he didn't have to decide today. In short, it helped him take a step back and widen his perspective, reminding him that current circumstances, although extremely challenging, would not last forever. This tool helped him navigate the crisis without burning out and realize that the professional path he was on was still the right one for him. He's still CEO today, successful and happy.

What if nothing comes to you when you try this exercise? What if you're unable to imagine your future self? No problem. Filmmaker Steven Spielberg, considered among the greatest directors of all times, often doesn't know ahead of time how exactly he's going to shoot a scene. You can create a vision the way a spider weaves its web: thread by thread. Each thread is something that resonates with you, whether images, words, sounds, places, or situations. If you were a song or a movie, which would it be? Or a tree? A color? And most important, *why*? What did you want to become when you were a child? Our child's brain, unconstrained because of its undeveloped frontal cortex, does this naturally, and everything feels possible. As we grow older and our rational, analytical abilities develop, our imagination recedes, and we get bogged down in the "can't" and "should." Imagination is a muscle: the more you flex it, the stronger it becomes. In any case, this is not a sprint. It can take time to figure out who you truly are and what you deeply want. So, pay attention to that resonance within you. Follow its lead, for it gives you clues that like breadcrumbs guide you home toward a truer, purer version of who you are and what you want.

I too was once unable to visualize my future. In Chapter 7, I share how becoming very ill made me realize with absolute certainty that I needed to make big changes in my life and gave me the courage and the space to do it, too. So, what was the right career, or even the right life, for me at that point? What kind of life would make me feel like me? Initially, I had absolutely no idea. I struggled to imagine myself in the future with enough specifics to act on. I realized later that I had stopped giving myself permission to dream, and like a muscle that is no longer used, my ability to do so had atrophied. I had to learn how to dream and imagine again.

I remember getting a whiteboard, which I hung over my bed. I would start collecting anything that inspired joy, happiness, excitement, or any other positive reaction, and I would keep following whatever path they opened. Initially, few images went up on the board. I relied on the things and people around me who supported me and could help me reconnect with myself. Little by little, the vision of what my own path of roses looked like became clearer and clearer in my mind. Then a new image made it to my whiteboard. Then another, and another. Ideas started popping into my head and new people crossed my path, seemingly out of nowhere. I followed one thread, which led to another. An initial idea for a business led nowhere, but in the process, I met other people or got other ideas that eventually led me to start my first company with a business partner I'd met during that exploration and visioning period.

It was also during that period that I came across a painting by Denis Frémond, part of his New York Cities series. Something clicked. The painting is of an interior, light flooding through a window that overlooks the city. Far in the background, on the side, a man stands. For reasons I cannot fully explain, that image deeply spoke to me. It felt like a visual metaphor of who I wanted to be. Today, years after I first saw that image, what initially felt like an echo has now fully manifested, and I have stepped into that vision of myself.

That period of my life reminds me of the words of psychiatrist Milton Erickson: "We don't know what our goals are. We learn our goals only in the process of getting there. You don't know what the baby is going to become. Therefore, you wait and take good care of it until it becomes what it will."[10]

Identify Your Role Models

Another way to identify who you want to be, particularly who you want to be as a leader, is to identify your role models and *why* they inspire you. As designer, writer, and coach Ayse Birsel points out, these are qualities you can embrace and develop in yourself.[11] So imagine being more like your role models. What would it look like in the context of your own life? What would it feel like? What can you do today to manifest these qualities?

When leadership coach Marshall Goldsmith was 14 years old, back in Kentucky, his father, Bill, hired a roofer named Dennis Mudd to fix the roof of the family home, which was leaking. The family didn't have much money, so to lower the repair cost, young Marshall was to help the roofer. Dennis Mudd was a dedicated roofer, and he showed Marshall the ropes and explained everything about roofs. When they were finished, Dennis Mudd called Marshall's dad to inspect the roof. "If the roof is of high quality," he said, "pay me. But if the quality is poor, this is free."

This left a lasting impression on young Marshall. "This man is poor," he thought of Dennis Mudd, "but he's not cheap. He has integrity and character. I want to be like him when I grow up!"

Some 15 years later, long before executive coaching became known as executive coaching, a 30-year-old Marshall Goldsmith was leading corporate training workshops as a consultant. At the end of a session, the CEO of the company approached him. He told Marshall about a young guy working for the company who was smart, dedicated, and driven. There was only one problem, the CEO explained—that guy was a jerk. He was arrogant and rude. "It would be worth a fortune to me if that guy could change," he sighed.

"I think maybe I can help him," Marshall said.

"I doubt it," the CEO replied, skeptical.

Marshall remembered Dennis Mudd. "I will work with him for a year," he offered. "If he gets better, pay me. And if he doesn't, it's all free!"

Can you guess what happened? The CEO agreed on the spot. The employee became Marshall's first individual client, and within the course of that year, he got better. Forty-four years later, Marshall still coaches top executives—and still remembers Dennis Mudd.[12]

Identifying who inspires us and why helps us define the kind of leader we want to be and what actions we can take today to be that person. Once he managed to let go of his father's and his professor's opinions, Andrew, for example, chose Nelson Mandela and Abraham Lincoln as his role models for leadership. Why? Because he felt that not only their ideas and values but also their humanity inspired people to follow them. In his eulogy, he'd written that he wanted to be remembered as someone who had the courage to be himself and could be counted on. Also important to him was to be remembered as someone who had helped others deploy their unique talents and inspired them to achieve more than they thought possible. Taken together, these exercises helped reveal who he wanted to be. Visualizing clearly what human leadership meant to him fueled his motivation to change and helped him identify clearly which behaviors he wanted to keep, which he wanted to develop, and those he wanted to drop. He would further develop and manifest his genuine care for and interest in his employees and their well-being and learn to become more patient and a better listener. He would rein in old reflexes to come up with solutions, and instead focus on creating an environment that inspired and enabled his teams to be and do more.

Actor Matthew McConaughey beautifully illustrates how imagining our future self can pull us forward and lift us up. When he was 15 years old, he was asked who his hero was. He thought about it. "It's me in 10 years," he eventually said. Then when asked the same question at age 25, his answer was the same. "You see, every day, and every week, and every month, and every year of my life, my hero is always 10 years away," he explains. "I'm never going to be my hero . . . and that's fine with me because it keeps me with somebody to keep on chasing."[13]

So flex your imagination muscle. Step into your future self to pull your present self forward. How does that work? It works because of how your brain works. When you imagine the future in vivid detail, your brain reacts as if you were living that life, triggering a cascade of neurotransmitters and hormones. It creates a "memory" of the future, which in turns affects your perspective and behavior today, spurring you into action.

In addition to pulling you forward onto your path of roses, flexing your imagination in this way carries multiple other benefits.

The Other Benefits of Flexing Your Imagination

Imagine living in a world in the grip of a global pandemic due to a new respiratory virus, which is rapidly spreading around the world. If I ask you now, several years after the outbreak of the COVID-19 pandemic, this doesn't seem like much of a stretch, does it? But what if you'd been asked to imagine such a world back in 2008?

This is exactly what Jane McGonigal, a game designer and futurist, did. Back in 2008, she asked nearly 10,000 people around the world to imagine themselves living 11 years into the future—fall 2019—when a pandemic due to a respiratory virus was quickly spreading around the world. What daily habits would they change? What problems would they face in their daily lives? How would they react faced with government-imposed quarantines? This is the kind of imagination flexing that scientists call *episodic future thinking*—EFT for short. The purpose of the simulation was to map what the economic, social, political, and emotional impact of global threats might be. Fast-forward to the COVID-19 pandemic—the real one, not the simulated one. People's actual behavior and emotional response mirrored what the simulation had predicted 12 years earlier.

This wasn't a random lucky guess. In 2010, Jane McGonigal ran another simulation involving some 20,000 participants, who were asked to imagine themselves in 2020. What situation did she ask them to envisage? Not only a global pandemic due to a respiratory virus but also conspiracy theories and disinformation spreading through social media, as well as several extreme events due to climate change, including wildfires on the West Coast of the United States and a collapse of the power grid. Does this combination of crises sound eerily familiar?

Yet Jane McGonigal argues the most meaningful role of such simulations isn't to accurately predict the future. It is to "prepare our minds and stretch our collective imagination, so we are more flexible, adaptable, agile, and resilient when the 'unthinkable' happens."[14] She has found that training our imagination through episodic future thinking, in addition to making us better at spotting clues of what might happen, brings unexpected gifts: it strengthens our mental health, protects our cognitive abilities, bolsters our motivation, and boosts our creativity.

Multiple studies have confirmed that people who flex their imagination toward specific future scenarios tend not only to be more optimistic but also less likely to feel anxious or depressed. How come? Without imagination, hoping for a better future isn't possible. Practicing EFT helps us control and channel our imagination so that it is neither too vague or inexistent, which is associated with depression, nor stuck in overdrive, which is related to anxiety. In addition to strengthening our mental health, training our ability to imagine future scenarios in detail also has cognitive benefits. A decline in that ability has been associated with conditions such as dementia, traumatic brain injuries, and post-traumatic stress. So exercises and games to improve that skill are being used in clinical environments.[15] Third, spending time training our brain to imagine our future vividly has also been shown to boost our motivation to do things *today* that carry long-term benefits—the pull factor discussed previously in this chapter. And finally, studies have shown that participants who were asked to imagine a situation in the future performed a lot better in creativity tests afterwards.[16]

In short, flexing our imagination helps us become more resilient to future shocks, but also be more creative in the present—all skills and qualities that make us better, more effective human leaders. It gives what is typically referred to as our "right brain," or the neural pathways associated with intuition, creativity, and emotions, space to expand—not literally of course, but figuratively—and taps into its natural ability to generate solutions that seem to appear out of nowhere.

* * *

Our imagination is our most powerful tool for change. When used properly, it helps clarify what's important to us, who we truly are and can be, and how we want to incorporate this into how we lead. By helping us understand and connect with what drives us and the kind of human leader we want to be, this part of the mindbuild creates our compass and the engine we need to keep walking on our path of roses and stay on track. If this were not reward enough, it is good for our health, too, and teaches us to prepare and plan for an unpredictable future. We'll see in Chapter 11 how exercising our brain in this way also helps us connect with others differently, which is at the heart of human leadership.

Vision without action, however, is nothing more than day-dream. Now that you've built a clear vision of the kind of human leader you can be, it is time to turn this vision into reality.

SELF-REFLECTION

1. **Understand what drives you**
   - What drives you?
   - Write your eulogy. What do you want others to say about you that day? How do you want to be remembered? Make sure you cover all parts of your life: family, friends, community, colleagues, and so on.

2. **Imagine your future self**
   - Pick an area of your current life that you'd like to change. Then imagine that anything is possible and visualize yourself in 10 years. What are you doing? Where are you? Whom are you with? How is that area of your life different?
   - Who are your role models? What specific qualities do you admire in them?
   - What can you do today to manifest these same qualities in your own life?
   - If you were a movie, a song, or a book, which one would you be and why?
   - What was your childhood dream and why?

3. **The other benefits of flexing your imagination**
   - Spend time imagining future scenarios in detail. Dream.

CHAPTER 10

Empower Your Inner Leader

Four Practices to Better Connect with Yourself

Smelling the sweet fragrance of roses, the child is about to embark on the path. Two wolves stand beside him. One is pulling him onto the path. The other is pulling him backwards.

"Which one will win?" the child asks.

The magician smiles. "The one you feed."

* * *

After shifting your mindtraps (Part 2) and adopting a new outlook, you're now on your path of roses. In Chapter 9, you decided how you want it to look and smell like. This is only the beginning, however. You need to keep walking and stay on course. And as you do, you need to care for it, keep the weeds out, feed the soil, and water the roses you've chosen. Mindbuilding requires the same consistent and regular approach so the new neural pathways you've now created can strengthen over time.

Bestselling authors Jim Collins and Morten T. Hansen tell the story of two teams of explorers that raced to the South Pole in 1911. They had similar experience and skills, had equivalent distances to cover, and faced similarly brutal conditions. The team led by explorer Roald Amundsen reached the South Pole first and returned home safely. The second, led by Robert Falcon Scott, arrived 34 days later to find their rival team's flag already planted, and they perished on the way back. The difference? Discipline and consistency. Amundsen's team walked 15–20 miles every single day, regardless of conditions: they pushed on through blizzards, but also stopped at 20 miles on good days when they could have walked more. The other adopted a different approach: when conditions were favorable, they marched until exhaustion, but on days when conditions were bad, they stayed in their tents.[1] The story illustrates the secret of reaching our objective in any journey, whether to the South Pole or toward becoming a human leader: work on it every day.

Strengthening new thought patterns and behavior takes adopting new habits, which require consistent repetition and practice. Building these consistent and daily habits is therefore the only way mindbuilding can be sustainable and lasting.

Unlike racing to the South Pole, however, a human leader's mindbuild is an ongoing journey and evolution with no finish line. It is a consistent and regular practice.

But what do these mindbuilding habits for human leaders involve exactly? They involve two things: learning to better keep in touch with ourselves, which is what this chapter focuses on, and learning to connect with others, which is what Chapter 11 is all about.

Our mindbuild's first practice is to maintain a daily check-in with ourselves for two main reasons:

- Make sure we stay on the right path.
- Take care of ourselves and recharge by drawing on positive memories, practicing gratitude, and learning to empathize without burning out.

There is a good reason why airlines ask passengers to first put on their own mask before assisting anyone else: we cannot help anyone, at least not for very long, if we can't breathe. The same is true with leadership. We cannot effectively lead others unless we properly lead ourselves first.

Staying on the Right Path

Every morning, John Donahoe, the CEO of Nike, spends time on what he calls "a workout of the mind," which includes both meditating and connecting with what he's grateful for.[2] So does Arianna Huffington.[3] Every evening when she drives home from work, Best Buy CEO Corie Barry spends a few minutes reminding herself of what drives her—leave the world a little bit better than when she found it—and what she's done that day that contributes to it. Eric Yuan, the CEO of Zoom, spends a few minutes every day reflecting about the day.

In Chapter 9, you clarified what drives you, which serves as your inner compass. You also identified the kind of leader you want to be, and how you want to behave. Yet staying in touch with your inner compass and whether your behavior aligns with who you want to be as a leader doesn't happen by itself. Staying in touch requires spending time with yourself daily. If the word *meditation* conjures up images of sitting in the lotus position or standing on your head, don't worry. All you have to do is take a few minutes every day to step back, remind yourself what matters to you most, how you've decided to change your behavior and why, and take stock of how you're doing on that score. In the 1997 movie *Good Will Hunting*, Robin Williams's baseball-loving character tells the story of how he decided to miss what turned out to be one of the biggest games in the Boston Red Sox's history because he "gotta go see about a girl." All of us mindbuilders are like Robin Williams, except we gotta go see about ourselves.

There are many ways to check in with ourselves, as the examples of leaders' own daily routines illustrate. Among these many ways, one I find particularly helpful is the practice of daily questions. How does that work? Remember the behaviors you've decided to keep, add, or drop, as well as the actions you've decided to take, to become who you want to be. Write them down, and at the end of each day, ask yourself whether you've done your best to behave and act accordingly. Just read the short list and answer yes or no, or give yourself a grade from 1 to 10.

At first, many clients of mine balk at this approach. "Doing your best is pointless," they argue. "Either you succeed, or you don't." But "Have I done my best today to . . ." is not about beating yourself up over the nos or getting 10s across the board. The main purpose of doing this is to quickly remind yourself and your brain that you've decided to think and behave in a certain way, and why it's important to you, so it doesn't get lost in the busyness of daily life. It is also to roughly measure your behavior and give you a sense of progression. During his daily self-reflection, Zoom's CEO Eric Yuan, for example, reviews the decisions he's made during the day and asks himself whether he really needed to make this or that decision himself, or whether his team should instead.[4] Over time, after being reminded every day through these daily check-ins, your brain will no longer need these prompts. And as it becomes second nature, the nos will become fewer, and the grades higher, which enable you to see and measure over time how much you've improved. Once again, the list of daily questions is about building a habit and about evolving, not about reaching a destination or being perfect. The list of questions itself is meant to evolve over time, along with your priorities and what you want to focus on.

If questions don't do it for you, try affirmations specifically tailored to what you've decided to work on to become the human leader you've envisioned. Have you endeavored to become more patient? Then remind yourself every day that you can be. Or have you decided to trust yourself more? Consider "I'm enough" as an affirmation, for example. What matters most is not so much the specifics of how you check in with yourself, whether you go through your list of daily questions and affirmations, meditate, or just take a few minutes to reflect. What matters is to do this every day, so it becomes a habit. *Every day? Who has time for this!* you might think. Yes, every day. Why? Remember that our neural pathways are like our muscles: unless they're exercised regularly and consistently, they weaken. Millions of things happen during the day, every day. Unless we build a daily habit of taking a step back, we fall back into the groove of how we've been thinking and operating, particularly when under pressure.

This is what happened to senior executive David when he went on a family holiday during the summer. By then, we'd been working together for several months, and he'd identified his main mindtrap and shifted it out of the way. After his holiday, however, he'd fallen back into negative thinking and old mental habits. His eyes had lost the inner light that shone through just a few weeks earlier. "Have you gone through your daily self-check-in while on holiday?" I asked him. He realized he'd initially skipped one day here and there. Then the occasional off-day became more frequent, until eventually, he forgot to do it altogether. Like a thermostat, he'd slid back to his old default mode.

So did senior executive Bruce. After shifting his mindtrap, he'd learned to delegate and listen more, be more open, and involve his teams in solving problems rather than issue directives from the top. Then his company was hit with a severe disruption of its supply chain, which turned into a major crisis. Under significant pressure and stress, Bruce fell back on his old behavior of making all the decisions and micromanaging, afraid that his team would not be able to handle the situation.

It takes time and persistence to build new habits. As your new neural pathways become stronger and your old ones weaken, these daily check-ins with yourself become faster and easier. I no longer need to remind myself to go through my own daily questions, for example. It has become an automatic part of my routine, like brushing my teeth. I've also added new questions and dropped others—our list is meant to change and evolve over time to reflect how we change and evolve over time, too. What remains constant is the practice.

Besides the daily check-ins, it is helpful to revisit the exercises in Chapter 9 occasionally. Is your personal *why* still the same? Does it still align with your company's and the work you do? What drove you and was most important to you 5, 10, or 20 years ago may be very different to what it is today. Your work or your company may have changed. The same is true of your role models and the way you imagine your future self: they may change, and so will the behaviors you want to focus on. Why? Because we're not snapshots frozen in time but human beings who keep evolving and changing.

So daily check-ins with yourself, as well as occasional longer-term ones, are essential to staying in touch with your inner compass and reminding yourself how you've decided to show up as a leader and why. But daily check-ins are also crucial to recharge and resource, which is critical self-care for human leaders.

Self-Care for the Soul

Do you remember the idea of draining versus energizing emotions introduced in Chapter 8? We all experience emotions such as stress, anxiety, or anger, which rob us of our energy. The combination of multiple complex crises, such as geopolitical tensions, social and economic challenges, and disrupted supply chains, have left many leaders on the verge of burnout. Fatigue and anxiety, however, make it difficult to lead effectively. How do you switch gears away from what drains you, and how do you recharge? Do you exercise or watch a movie? Read or meditate? Listen or play music perhaps? Everyone's bag of tools looks different. Following are a few suggestions to explore and expand yours.

Draw from a Bank of Positive Memories

In times of stress or fatigue, imagination and visualizations are once again helpful. But in this instance, you're using your imagination to recharge. Create a bank of your favorite places—places that you know and are associated with positive emotions for you. Instead of places, you can create a collection of positive memories. Thanks to your imagination, you can take yourself there any time you want to recharge.

During my years as an entrepreneur, for example, whenever the company's funding was tight, and we faced seemingly insurmountable hurdles, I visualized walking on my favorite beach at sunrise. I could feel sunrays warming my skin, a soft ocean breeze, and salt water gently brushing my feet. In my mind, I would sit by a rock, looking at the light dancing on the calm water surface, listening to the faint cry of seagulls. Sometimes a pod of dolphins would swim by. As my chest filled with joy and calm, I was able to remember that my job wasn't to singlehand-edly fix all our problems, but instead to mobilize our collective energy and power as a team so we could work out solutions—something I was confident I could do.

One of my clients picked his favorite place in the Caribbean, where he'd been on holidays. In his mind's eye, he pictured him-self basking in a beam of sunlight over the water. Whenever a storm approached and the ocean became choppy, he would grab a trapeze to lift above the waves. Another client, an avid surfer, keeps surfing photos on his desk, so he can connect with the freedom and joy he feels whenever he catches some waves. Some people prefer to travel back to specific memories that fill them with energy or joy, moments they shared with their family or their friends. Several clients have even made short videos of happy moments—their children laughing, a group of friends chatting over dinner—which they can play every time they need a boost.

Practice Gratitude

There is a very scientific reason behind this practice: many neu-rological studies have confirmed its impact on our brain on multiple levels, affecting neurotransmitters, stress hormones and even neural structures.[5] By helping us release stress and boosting a sense of well-being, being grateful therefore helps us recharge. Besides having a remarkable impact on our own well-being, practicing gratitude also greatly affects our ability to lead other people and deliver surprising results, as leadership experts Adrian Gostick and Chester Elton have illustrated in more detail in a recent book—more on this in Chapter 11.[6]

Why do we need to practice it, though? Because our brains are wired to focus on problems and dangers, and therefore are naturally drawn to noticing the negative more than the positive. Correcting this neurological bias therefore requires practice. All it takes is a few seconds to bring our attention to a few things that we're grateful for. These could be as simple as the color of the sky in that moment or a smile from a stranger. The important part is to connect deeply and genuinely with the emotion of appreciation itself, which is what changes our brain structure. So, try to pick different reasons every day to feel grateful, so you have to actively think and remind yourself of something that perhaps you would otherwise not have noticed or remembered, overshadowed by all the small or big challenges that every day brings.

The simple act of smiling helps put us in touch with a feeling of gratitude that uplifts and energizes us. Try it now. Just stretch the corners of your mouth toward your ears. Do it in a relaxed manner, so it becomes a genuine smile, rather than a rictus. Do you notice how your mood changes, just through this simple action?

But wait. Isn't dissatisfaction a powerful motivator? Doesn't feeling grateful risk blunting our own drive? No. Being grateful doesn't mean that we suddenly become blind to problems and what we want to improve. We can be grateful *and* want better or more at the same time.

Another related tool is what is known as "empathic joy." Much like practicing to notice things we appreciate to develop gratitude, we can also flex our empathy to notice and connect with other people's joy. Psychologist and Stanford University lecturer Kelly McGonigal points out that connecting to other people's challenging emotions, whether stress or pain, is more instinctive than connecting to their positive ones; but by practicing noticing moments of happiness around us, we learn to cultivate empathic joy, or, as she puts it, to "catch joy," which helps us recharge.[7]

In addition to recharging by shifting draining emotions and practicing gratitude, another element of self-care for human leaders is to make sure that we don't drown in other people's emotions.

Learn to Protect Yourself and Recharge

Think of a cup of tea: if you pour milk in it, it mixes in with the hot water. But if you pour oil, it floats on the surface. The objective is for us to float like the oil, so we don't get mixed up and drown in other people's perspectives and emotions.

There can be no helpful empathy without self-protection. Without the ability and time to come back to yourself, being able to connect with someone else to see the world through their eyes and feel what they experience—what I define as empathy—can lead to emotional saturation, particularly during challenging circumstances. That saturation in turn can result in our switching off empathy altogether. This is something doctors, nurses, and other care professionals know well: when faced with too much grief and tragedy among their patients, they risk building emotional walls to protect themselves. But when this protection becomes extreme, they're no longer able to connect with patients, which makes them less effective at their job. It is a question of balance. The best doctors can connect with their patients and understand their pain, but also detach enough to get back to their expertise to diagnose and ease their ailments, as well as protect themselves.[8] The best leaders are also able to connect with all their stakeholders and understand them, but also to come back to their role and perspective.

Developing our ability to connect with others means that we also risk absorbing their perspectives, moods, and emotions. But this is not helpful to us or to them, because we cannot help from that position. Also, as we've illustrated in this book, this muddles our own voice. So the objective is to strike a fine balance between connecting with others so we can understand them, and also being able to come back to ourselves. But how do we do that? Whenever we need to leave perspectives and emotions that belong to other people with them, simple physical gestures can help. Close your eyes and bring your hands together in front of your solar plexus. Imagine all these external influences—whether words, behavior, or emotions—that have come into your own mental space floating in the space immediately in front of you. Then cut through them by extending your arms in front of you, palms still against each other, and move your arms as if swimming breast-stroke, pushing everything that doesn't belong to you to the side and then behind you—and out of our own mental space. That way, you free the space in front of you and you can breathe better. This exercise can be practiced physically, but you can also visualize yourself doing it.

You can also imagine a protective bubble around you, against which these words and emotions bounce off back to their source without reaching you. Make that bubble transparent, so you can still see everything and everyone around you.

Physical exercise is also helpful to come back to yourself and leave behind emotions you might have picked up from other people. Many of my clients also listen to some of their favorite songs or music every day, which helps them come back to themselves and recharge their emotional batteries. Others find nature re-energizing. Find what helps you recharge the most, and make sure to include it in your daily routine—whether it's going for a run, listening to a few songs, or taking a few minutes to stroll in your garden or a city park on your way to or from the office.

Self-care also means knowing when to get help and where to get it. Whether it is with a therapist, a coach, a group of peers, friends and family, or a spiritual leader, effective human leaders know how to openly ask for help when they need it and explore their emotions so they're able to create and maintain a safe, open, and supporting environment at work for their teams.

* * *

In this chapter, we've shared tools to build and maintain a daily practice of keeping in touch with ourselves. But this isn't the only element of our ongoing mindbuild practice. The main reason for staying on the path we've set for ourselves and practicing self-care through the exercises laid out is this: unless we're first solidly connected with ourselves, we cannot properly connect with others, which is at the heart of human leadership.

Fundamental to being an effective human leader is learning to better connect with others, which is what Chapter 11 is about.

SELF-REFLECTION

Create a daily routine to catch up with yourself. Following are some steps to get you started.

1. Staying on the right path

- Write down the key behaviors that you've decided to change. Write them somewhere that you can easily access from anywhere, such as your cell phone.

- Make an appointment with yourself every day. Select the most appropriate time for you.

2. Self-care for the soul

- What are specific moments that filled you with happiness and joy? Make a list. Go back to them whenever you need.

- Find three things for which you're grateful today. Repeat every day.

- What do you do to refuel? What gives you joy? How often do you do it?

- Whom do you talk to when you need emotional support?

CHAPTER 11

Become a New Leader

Four Practices to Better Connect with Others

While walking on his own path of roses, the child notices that every flower is different. Taking a closer look, the child observes that some are in full bloom, others still small buds. Some grow in the shade, others in full sunlight. Some need watering, others not. Some need pruning, others fertilizer. The child learns to observe the flowers every day and be attentive to what they each need to grow and blossom. The child understands that caring for each rose changes with the seasons and the weather, too. So he learns to listen to the wind, to notice whether the air is hot or cool, and to look out for clouds on the horizon and anticipate rain. As the child moves forward, he keeps learning how to become a better gardener.

And every day when meeting with a rose, he asks, "How do you feel today? Do you need anything?"

"Thank you for asking!" the rose beams. "I feel respected and loved, so for now, I can grow safely."

And so the child goes, walking forward on his path of roses, feeling richer and happier for having unlocked his human gift.

* * *

In addition to connecting with ourselves, extending our mindbuilding practice to better connect with others takes time and consistent practice, too. Deciding, for example, to be a leader who embraces authentic relationships and unleashes other people's potential, rather than one bent on proving we're smarter than everyone else, does not mean we know how to do this from day one.

Think of your own body. How do you become and stay fit? Do you exercise once and miraculously stay strong for the rest of your life? No. To build and maintain muscles and cardio fitness, you need to exercise very regularly and consistently; if you stay immobile, your muscles, including your heart, will weaken. Mindbuilding is like bodybuilding, because your neural pathways are exactly like your muscles: they need to be exercised consistently and regularly to grow stronger over time. In short, it's a case of "use 'em or lose 'em."

In Chapter 9, you imagined your future self and identified role models to clarify what kind of leader you want to be. Regardless of the specifics, which are unique to you, being an effective human leader starts with being able to genuinely connect with others. As Theodore Roosevelt pointed out, "No one cares how much you know, until they know how much you care." Following are four practices to strengthen your ability to connect with others:

- Learn to listen more and speak last.
- Cultivate your empathy.
- Practice and role-play conversations.
- Learn to set and maintain new boundaries.

Learn to Listen More and Speak Last

The most effective human leaders are those who have successfully repositioned their role from quarterback to coach. Their job is no longer to handle the ball and score points; it is to inspire and support the players to give the best of themselves and make sure they play as a team so together they can score points. In other words, leading requires different attributes and behaviors than managing. Learning how to move from one to the other is not easy: early in a career, success often depends on knowing how to be a good quarterback. In a leadership position, however, knowing how to ask questions is more important than coming up with answers. In *The Coaching Habit*, leadership coach Michael

Bungay Stanier offers a framework of seven essential questions to change how we lead.[1] Similarly, speaking last is more effective for leaders than volunteering ideas and opinions first. In other words, one of the essential qualities of effective human leadership is knowing how to listen. Becoming an excellent listener is critical not only in itself but also because it underpins other elements essential to being an effective human leader, such as empathy—more on this in a later section.

Hubert Joly experienced firsthand how hard it can be to make that transition from quarterback to coach. When he headed Carlson Wagonlit Travel, the head of human resources handed him a new org chart at a company party. The new chart was peculiar: the name that appeared in every box was Hubert's. The joke was revealing, though. By his own account, Hubert Joly had been jumping in to solve his teams' problem for years and, without even realizing it, telling them what to do. After all, wasn't it exactly why he'd become CEO?

The problem was he hadn't yet repositioned himself as a leader.[2]

By the time he became CEO of Best Buy, the electronic retailing chain that was then on the verge of a precipice, Hubert Joly approached his role very differently. He spent his first few days on the job working in a Best Buy store, observing and asking everyone who worked there a lot of questions. He then mobilized a team of some 30 people from all parts of the business to create a turnaround plan. How did he approach his own role? Ask questions, listen, and create the right conditions so everyone could come up with answers together and co-create a plan.

He credits his change of approach to several things, including some coaching. But what also helped greatly was being an outsider with no experience in retail. He knew he didn't know and had a lot to learn. There was no temptation to jump in and try to fix everything because he was new to the company and new to the sector. This is the silver lining of confronting multiple complex and unprecedented crises, as leaders do today: there is no expertise or experience to fall back on and contribute, which makes it easier to step back, reposition, and behave as a human leader. "It's easier to say 'I don't know' when we actually don't know," Hubert Joly points out.[3]

How do we become better listeners?

As a child and teenager, Bob Dylan spent nights listening to anything that came out of the radio. There was R&B, jazz, gospel, and rock 'n roll. But he was also fascinated by radio dramas. This is how he learned to listen to small, random, everyday things like a door slamming or the whistling of wind through the trees. "It made me listen to life in a different way," he said later. "It made me the listener that I am today."[4]

Like anything else, changing behavior starts with intention and mindset: adopting a learn-it-all mindset rather than a know-it-all attitude, to borrow Microsoft CEO Satya Nadella's words, goes a long way in helping shift our behavior from speaking to listening. Showing how much we know typically involves speaking; wanting to learn, however, shifts our behavior toward asking questions and listening. A learn-it-all mindset, coupled with the ability to listen, also helps human leaders own and acknowledge their own mistakes. Nadella, shortly after becoming CEO, was asked during a conference what advice he would give women uncomfortable asking for pay raises. His answer to "have faith in the system" instead of asking for pay rises unleashed a furore.[5] His learn-it-all mindset, his authenticity, and his ability to listen meant he could quickly and easily acknowledge that he'd answered the question "completely wrong" and that he'd learned "a valuable lesson."[6] This signaled within Microsoft that no one, including the CEO, was expected to be infallible. Mary Barra, the CEO of General Motors, sums up this mindset: "It's okay to admit what you don't know. It's okay to ask for help. And it's more than okay to listen to the people you lead. In fact, it's essential."[7]

Speaking last helps leaders become better listeners, too. This is what I often advise my clients who struggle to stop themselves from jumping in to fix problems that others are perfectly capable of handling if given a chance: turn your tongue in your mouth six times before speaking or count to 10.

As trite as it may sound, we learn to listen by speaking less, too, in addition to speaking last. Musician Greta Morgan found that out the hard way. In 2020, she was diagnosed with a rare neurological disorder that affected her voice permanently. She could no longer hold a note, her voice was wavering uncontrollably, and her vocal range had dramatically narrowed. For someone who makes living as a lead singer, this was devastating, and she experienced what she described as "identity death." She retreated to Springdale just outside Zion Canyon National Park for a month to rest her voice completely. And as she stopped talking, something unexpected happened: she started really listening and realized how much more she could hear. "It was as if I had never listened in my life," she remembers. It transformed the way she paid attention to the world around her.[8]

Learning to listen also means learning to be mentally present. Whenever we're thinking about our last meeting or the next one, or checking our phones, we're not properly listening, even if we don't say a word. Learning to listen to others, really listen to them, requires complete focus. How can we do that when the human brain automatically produces a constant tsunami of thoughts? It takes practice. Mindfulness—in other words, being fully present—has been shown through countless studies to help us quiet our mind—and a quiet mind is a listening mind. This doesn't have to be complicated: I often advise my clients to practice what I call the "close the door and open the door" exercise: at the end of each meeting, conversation, or activity, resist the temptation to jump straight into the next one. Instead, take a moment to close the door on what you've just done, so you don't carry on thinking about it as you start your next conversation or undertaking. Closing that door could mean jotting down a few notes and thoughts or scheduling some time to think about it more so you're able to set it aside and empty your mind. Or it could mean doing nothing more than taking a few seconds or one minute to bring your mind into the present, interrupting the flow of thoughts about what did happen or will happen or should happen.

It is sometimes helpful to associate this mental discipline with a ritual: it could be as simple as drinking a glass of water, walking one lap around your office, or taking a few deep breaths—anything that, over time, will act as your own mental circuit breaker. For some of my clients, this circuit breaker is taking a few minutes to drink a cup of coffee or looking out the window. Then you "open the door," which means you bring your full attention to what comes next in your schedule.

Staying present and truly listening is also easier when we're able to let go of our own agenda. For many leaders, letting go of our agenda means letting go of the noble and understandable, but at times counterproductive, desire for every conversation to be productive. By "productive," I mean conversations with a predetermined agenda that not only gets tackled from the get-go but also discussions that produce a decision, whether some kind of fix or at least next steps. I'm not saying that time management and focus aren't important; they are, of course, particularly when days are packed and time is precious. What I mean is learning to relate to colleagues as people is equally important and a productive use of time: people who don't feel heard at work don't feel respected and included so they typically don't invest much of themselves into their job and, of course, aren't the best version of themselves. It is about finding a balance. What about taking a few minutes at the beginning of a meeting to check in and find out how people are doing? What about spending a little time just catching up, with no agenda and without wanting to fix?

This is not easy. It takes practice and patience to know when to stop ourselves from rushing. At the height of the COVID-19 pandemic, for example, Andrew realized that members of his team felt isolated. Even though they attended strings of back-to-back Zoom meetings, they'd lost the human connection that popping into someone's office or chatting over coffee created. At the risk of adding to the video meeting fatigue, he introduced what can be described as coffee e-breaks—Zoom catch-ups with no specific work agenda, during which everyone on his team could check in with each other and get and offer support if needed.

In addition to letting go of our agenda, suspending our own judgment also helps us become better at what is known in Buddhism as "deep listening." As soon as we react to what someone else is saying, even if only in our head, then we can no longer truly listen. We get distracted by the "noise" of our own thoughts about how wrong, misguided, or unfair the other person might be, and our irritation or anger. For most of us, however, suspending judgment isn't a standard feature in our mental makeup, and it takes regular and consistent practice.[9]

Leaders who keep practicing becoming better listeners develop deeper and stronger connections with their teams, which in turn contributes to boosting their engagement and performance. Learning to listen better, however, is only one aspect of deepening and strengthening these connections. A second critical element, which in fact builds on listening, is to cultivate empathy.

Cultivate Your Empathy

The entire journey laid out in this book so far has already exercised the empathy muscle. Remember what I mean by empathy: the ability to connect to other people's emotions or experience. Being able to stand in someone's shoes, see the world through their eyes, and feel what they experience isn't about learning and applying a few party tricks. To be authentic and genuine, empathy must come from within. Think of it as *in-pathy*. Identifying your mindtrap(s), shifting it or them out of the way, and building and maintaining your new mindset creates an inner transformation that makes this *in-pathy* possible. In short, by traveling the mindtrap-mindshift-mindbuild journey, you've already upgraded your inner operating system, so your empathy function runs better.

So why bother with this section, then? This section is about how you can strengthen your empathy muscle, now that you've done the inner work required for that muscle to work at all. As surprising as this idea might sound at first, empathy is not a fixed attribute but a quality that can be learned and strengthened over time—just like learning to play piano or tennis. Except for a small minority of people, our brains are all wired for empathy. And even though we each start in life with varying levels of natural wiring, we can all build up our empathy neural pathways over time—with proper practice.

What does this practice look like, in addition to listening properly? Studies based on brain imaging have shown that regular practice of a specific type of meditation focused on empathy strengthens and activates the areas of the brain used to detect emotions and feelings.[10] So does looking for areas we have in common with someone else—rather than focusing on how different they are from us.

Another tool, in addition to becoming a better listener and meditation, is to practice hearing what is not being said. How? One very effective way is to practice communicating without words. One of the most enlightening experiences I've had in this regard was a leadership retreat I attended at The Horse Institute in upstate New York.[11] The retreat had nothing to do with riding horses—in fact, we didn't get on horseback at all; it was all about coaching participants to become better leaders through a technique known as equine-assisted learning. During one of the exercises, participants working in teams of three had to lead a horse so it would walk twice around a white square drawn on the ground, step inside the square, and then stop. The team members first spoke to each other to elaborate a plan of action and get on the same page for their shared goal.

Sounds easy enough, doesn't it? It isn't so easy when trying to do this with no rope and no verbal command to the horse, and no speaking to each other once setting foot in the ring. The only tool available is nonverbal connection—with the horse and with other team members. Because your horse is unable to *tell* you how it feels, you learn to connect and communicate in other ways: by observing its body language and its actions. Where are its ears facing? Is it shaking its head or looking at you? What are its eyes saying to you? Have you grabbed its attention? The idea is also to force the human participants to observe each other's actions and body language, because they're not allowed to speak.

Cultivating empathy also means remembering that its power runs both ways. In other words, it means understanding, when in a position of leadership, how your words, but also the tone of your voice, your body language, and your actions, affect your connections to the people around you. "The people around you" are not only the members of *your* immediate team but also, through them, the members of *their* immediate team. So, if you're in a position of top leadership, "the people around you" means *everyone* in the company. Therefore, once you observe and understand the impact of your words, your body language, and your actions, your empathy practice also includes adjusting what you say, how you say it, and what you do accordingly. This is why communicating in person or at least via video message is preferable to, say, email, which offers none of the nonverbal cues that are critical to human connection.

Let's go back to the horse retreat and the white square exercise. Connecting with the horse's emotions is only half the exercise. The other part is to figure out how, through your own body language and actions, you can lead the horse. If the horse is nervous, for example, how can you adjust your own emotions and behavior in a way that strengthens your connection so the horse trusts you? Or if your horse is distracted, how can you redirect its focus? And once the connection is established, how do you leverage it to communicate to the horse where it is meant to go and what it is supposed to do? How far or how close should you stand? Should you be in front or by its side? Where should you look? Which direction should you face? And what happens if the horse senses that you're irritated, frustrated, or nervous?

The beauty of this practice—and its challenge, too—is there is no universal recipe. Each horse, each human participant, and therefore the connection they establish between them, is unique. What works with some pairs at a precise moment may not with another horse, or the next day. The point is to learn to connect better and faster, and to maintain that connection. The same is true with human connection. Every individual is exquisitely unique—what drives them, what they need, what they want, and how they react—and so is every moment of every day. Sharpening your empathy is about deploying emotional energy and focus toward learning to adapt to every individual and every moment.

The point of the retreat is also to experience how powerful emotional connection is. Can't you lead a horse by putting a bit in its mouth, pulling on the reins, and giving it verbal cues? Isn't it a lot faster and easier? Perhaps, but this method only takes you so far. First, the horse is far heavier and stronger than you, so if it wants to stop responding, it will. More important, leading in that way is also far less effective and sustainable. The less you're able to connect with your horse, the harder you must pull on the reins and the louder you must speak. In short, the less empathetic we are as leaders, the more energy we must spend, often for poorer results. The horse exercise provides a direct and powerful experience of how exhilarating it becomes to lead by relying on emotional connection instead: it is like cycling with a strong wind at your back, instead of facing it. This experience, in turn, makes it crystal clear why it is worth investing time and effort practicing empathy.

Empathy shouldn't be confused with some touchy-feely, mushy sentiment. Being able to connect to someone else and experience the world from their perspective doesn't mean accepting or excusing everything they do or say. Empathy doesn't exclude

showing tough love whenever necessary. Consider what Microsoft CEO Satya Nadella told 150 company executives, for example.
"Once you become a vice president, a partner in this endeavor,
the whining is over. You can't say the coffee around here is bad, or
there aren't enough good people, or I didn't get the bonus. To be a
leader in this company, your job is to find the rose petals in a pile
of shit. You are the champions of overcoming constraints."[12]

Practice and Role-Play Conversations

Practice is about developing and reinforcing new habits.
Remember the first time you tried to ride a bicycle as a child. It
probably felt strange and unnatural. You initially had to focus on
every move, practicing what to do with your legs and your arms,
how to balance. No one expected you to do it perfectly from day
one. You practiced until it became natural, and you no longer
had to remind yourself to push down the pedals with your feet.

Changing how we connect with people at work might feel
awkward at first, even intimidating. More granular practice,
role-play, and guidance help make it easier over time. My client,
Bruce, for example, decided to organize a get-to-know-each-
other workshop with his team. The objective was for everyone
to share something meaningful about themselves and their story
that their colleagues didn't know, which would shed some light
on who they were and what drove them, and would help their
colleagues understand them better. To help everyone, including
my client, prepare and come up with something meaningful and
specific, questions were sent ahead of time, such as what is one
of your happiest memories, and why? What was the most challenging moment in your life, and why, and how did it shape you?
What is your dream and why? What drives you, what is important to you? Everyone had 10 minutes to share the story they'd
chosen and could choose how to share it.

Bruce was nervous: he'd never interacted with his team like that. What should he say? And how should he say it? I first worked with him on what he felt comfortable sharing. Which story should he pick and why? And how should he tell it? What were the relevant elements? How did this inform who he was today, and what drove him? How did that connect with his work at the company and how he approached it? He wrote it all down. Then he practiced with me how he would tell the story. On the day of the workshop, he kicked off with his own story to set the tone and put everyone else at ease. Then some people spent their own 10 minutes just talking, while others also shared videos, photos, or music. That workshop changed the dynamic within the team, fostering closer connections, as well as deeper understanding and respect. Having practiced before the event, Bruce felt more relaxed on the day, because although being vulnerable and interacting with his team in an entirely new way was completely new to him, he was prepared. Having practiced also reminded him why he was doing this, and why it was important.

This kind of simulation training made an enormous difference for US fighter pilots. In "Humans Are Underrated," Geoff Colvin tells the story of how the US Navy rethought how it trained its pilots during the Vietnam War, and the Air Force didn't. The Navy introduced combat simulations that mimicked "dogfights" as realistically as possible and were recorded so they could be reviewed and discussed afterwards. If you're a Tom Cruise fan, you already know that training program, known as Top Gun. The Air Force, however, continued with its traditional, mostly theoretical training approach. By the end of the war, the kill ratio of Air Force fighter pilots had slightly declined, whereas the Navy pilots' had tripled, even though they used the same jets. This confirmed that skills were far more important than technology. And thanks to their simulation training, the Navy fighter pilots had become much better at discerning and responding to what was in opposing pilots' minds during a dogfight, even though they couldn't even see them. In other words, they'd become elite pilots by developing their empathy, which turned out to be a critical factor in their success. As Air Force Colonel John Boyd pointed out, "Machines don't fight wars, people do, and they use their mind."[13] Few people might call the Navy pilots' training an exercise in empathy in this context, but that's nonetheless what it is.

I often role-play conversations with my clients—particularly conversations they expect to be difficult—or specific situations. "What should I say and what should I do if someone has just lost a loved one?" one client asked me during the worst of the COVID-19 pandemic. Imagine that your best friend is in this situation, I usually say. What would you tell him or her? What would you do?

Role-playing various scenarios eases the anxiety of the unknown and makes it easier to react in the best possible way in the heat of the moment. This is why elite military units spend time planning for contingencies and going over scenarios before every mission: when we're in fight-or-flight mode, parts of our brains shut down, making it much harder to think clearly and decide how best to react. Although our average day at the office doesn't involve life-and-death situations, our brains still go into varying levels of fight-or-flight mode when we face unfamiliar situations—such as learning to react to emotional situations.

Practicing and role-playing are also helpful when learning to show appreciation. Most leaders agree that showing appreciation is central to keeping people motivated; few people are happy to invest their time, effort, and creativity in an environment where their efforts and contribution go unnoticed. Yet leadership experts Adrian Gostick and Chester Elton have found that many leaders do not know how to show gratitude in a way that makes employees feel genuinely appreciated. In short, most workplaces suffer from what they call a gratitude gap. Showing appreciation is not about cranking up blanket thank-yous and telling people how great they are. To work its magic, appreciation must be authentic, specific, and timely. It's about noticing and understanding each individual's specific contributions, as well as the challenges they face. It's not about being nice or touchy-feely: leaders can be demanding and also know how to give specific, timely and authentic appreciation and credit where credit is due. But it takes practice.[14] So rein in the bland and generic thankyous and instead practice showing meaningful appreciation.

Over time, as we become more experienced developing and maintaining more human connections at work, we no longer need to practice in the same way, as we can automatically tap into the deep well of our memory instead.

Learn to Set and Maintain New Boundaries

Author and researcher Brené Brown once had a conversation with the CEO of a newly funded company from Silicon Valley. He was going to be vulnerable and authentic, he said to her. He would tell his employees and investors how the company was bleeding money, and that he had no idea what he was doing.

She reminded him that, although being vulnerable and authentic is indeed extraordinarily powerful for leaders, there is one critical caveat: vulnerability without boundaries is not vulnerability. If he genuinely felt in over his head, she added, he should indeed tell someone. But his investors and employees were the wrong people to talk to.

A lot has been said, written, and argued about why being authentic and vulnerable fosters genuine human connection. If we want to truly connect with other people, we must be ready to let them peek into our head and into our heart and encourage them to do the same. We must be ready and able to show who we truly are. This is where the power of authenticity and vulnerability lies for leaders: they are essential ingredients of human leadership because it is by creating and maintaining human connections that leaders can most inspire and motivate others. This is the payoff and why it is worth the risk and effort for leaders to learn to become more vulnerable and more authentic.

Opening a door so people at work can peek into our head and our heart, however, doesn't mean sharing all our emotions and all our thoughts with everybody. It also doesn't mean abandoning our privacy or forcing colleagues and team members to let go of theirs. This is a common perception among my clients, who worry becoming more vulnerable at work and encouraging others to do the same will turn a professional environment into a giant group therapy session. Indeed, without setting proper boundaries, vulnerability and authenticity at work are neither powerful nor productive, but exactly the opposite. Like in the story of Goldilocks and the three bears, there is a fine line between "too little" and "just right," and there is another one between "just right," and "too much."

So, where are these invisible lines when it comes to human leadership? How and where should human leaders set boundaries?

These boundaries look different for each one of us. Here are several questions to help you find yours:

1. **Is this relevant?** Being vulnerable doesn't mean sharing anything personal just for the sake of it. When Microsoft CEO Satya Nadella talks about his and wife's experience of having a son born with cerebral palsy, there is a clear purpose behind his story that is relevant well beyond its personal aspect. This is not a story about how unfair life can be or how everyone has problems. This is the story of how he learned empathy. Also, why he tells that story makes it eminently pertinent to Microsoft's employees, customers, and investors. He moves on from the personal angle to why empathy is a business imperative: to succeed, companies must understand their customers and their perspective, what they need

even when they cannot articulate it, and how these needs can be met. Through a personal story, Satya Nadella says a lot about who he is as a father and husband. But more important for anyone outside his family, he also says a lot about the kind of business leader he is, and what Microsoft stands for: since Satya Nadella became CEO in 2014, empathy—in other words, customer centricity—has been a central plank of Microsoft's business strategy, which has led to the company's renewal and success.[15]

So before telling a personal story or sharing how you feel, ask yourself *why* you're telling that story. What is the message you want to share? Is it something that is strictly about yourself and with no further relevance? If so, it probably doesn't belong to a work setting. Or is it relevant to your work or the company?

2. **Is it helpful?** Effective human leaders do not lose sight that the point of being authentic and vulnerable is to support, encourage, and motivate people by creating and strengthening human connections. Offloading your anxiety or frustration onto your colleagues in the name of authenticity may make you feel better, but that kind of authenticity isn't helpful to anyone else and therefore defeats the purpose. To be powerful, the emotions, thoughts, or stories that leaders share are meant to uplift, enlighten, or encourage others. When suggesting that human leaders should learn to say they don't know and ask for help, the idea is to say it and do it in a way that mobilizes and galvanizes people to work together and support each other. Sharing about yourself without showing interest in, and care for, others doesn't strengthen human connections: it only screams, "me, me, me!"

So, as Brené Brown so eloquently puts it, just ask yourself, "Are you sharing your emotions and your experiences to move your work, connection, or relationship forward? Or are you working your s—t out with somebody?"[16] If your answer to the second question is yes, then remember, as she pointed out to the Silicon Valley entrepreneur in the previous story, that work is not a place to do that.

3. **Am I undermining my competence as a leader?** "When we broadcast our limitations, we need to be careful to avoid casting doubt on our strengths," says organizational psychologist and author Adam Grant.[17] Unfair as it is, this is particularly true for women leaders. Saying you're out of your depth or worried about the future, like the Silicon Valley entrepreneur, is likely to fill your team with anxiety and make them wonder whether you should be in charge and why they should follow your lead. Asking for help to become better at what you do, however, sends the message that you're not perfect but that you're keen to keep improving. This typically makes other people want to help you. The coaching practice of "feedforward" does this beautifully. It involves first collecting feedback from your direct reports. After thanking your team for their contributions, you then choose two or three areas you'd like to work on and improve, before enrolling your team's help. Creating and maintaining proper boundaries is knowing when, how, and from whom to ask for help, and what for.

4. **Am I still feeling professional and comfortable?** We all maintain different boundaries when it comes to privacy. Being authentic and vulnerable is far more about how we show up than how much information we disclose.

"Some of the most vulnerable and authentic leaders I've ever had the pleasure of working with—truly authentic and truly vulnerable people—personally disclose very little," says Brené Brown. "And some of the leaders I work with disclose everything, and they are the least authentic and vulnerable people."[18]

If you're sharing more than you're comfortable with, you're no longer authentic. Instead of being yourself, you become someone who's trying too hard to be vulnerable—which, ironically, comes across as painfully inauthentic.

* * *

This chapter is the culmination of all the chapters that have come before. The inner work you've done—identifying your mindtrap(s) (Part 1), shifting these inner obstacles out of the way (Part 2), and building new habits to better keep in touch with yourself and your new mindset (Chapter 10)—has set the foundations for showing up as a new kind of leader: an authentic human leader not only willing but now also able to lead with empathy. Building on this inner work, this chapter has given you tools to better connect with people around you so you can lead from that place of human connection.

The tools in this chapter don't offer a shortcut: they don't by themselves magically transform a superhero leader into a human leader. The ability to lead with empathy comes from within, so applying these tools without the proper internal foundation invariably comes across as pretending to be a human leader, rather than being one. Conversely, inner work by itself is self-help, not human leadership. It becomes human leadership only when we learn and practice how to translate it into better connecting with others. Human leadership is born out of the combination of both these inner and outer dimensions—like an operating system and software working in tandem.

Although this is the last chapter of this book, this isn't the end of your journey as a human leader. In fact, this is only the beginning. As I tell the executives I coach, the mindtrap and mindshift parts of the journey can happen quickly; mindbuilding, however, is a practice. And as such, it is meant to happen for the rest of your life.

SELF-REFLECTION

1. Learn to listen more and speak last

- How much and when do you speak during meetings with your team?
- How often do you ask your team what support they need?
- Are you comfortable publicly acknowledging your mistakes?
- Are you comfortable saying "I don't know" and asking for help?

2. Cultivate your empathy

- Do you observe people's body language during conversations?
- Are you aware of your own body language during conversations?
- What is your main way of communicating with your team? Face-to-face or video meetings? Emails? Video or voice recordings?
- How do you anticipate others' reactions/needs?

3. Practice and role-play conversations

- Do you practice conversations that you expect to be challenging? If so, how?
- Do you organize structured opportunities for your team members, including yourself, to share something meaningful about themselves?
- How do you show appreciation toward others? Are you specific, authentic, and timely?

4. Learn to set and maintain new boundaries

- What does vulnerability mean to you in a work context?
- Before sharing anything at work, do you ask yourself the following questions:
  - Is this relevant to the situation?
  - Is it useful to others?
  - Am I undermining my competence as a leader?
  - Am I still feeling professional and comfortable?

Conclusion:
The New Leader

The journey from mindtrap to mindshift and mindbuild has a profound impact on those who undertake it, unleashing a deep and lasting transformation on multiple levels.

Take Andrew, the CEO whose oral exam in business school had shaped his views on leadership. After we identified his mindtrap and replaced it with a new perspective, he started looking at his role—and himself—completely differently. He gradually learned how to really listen and to be comfortable relating to employees on a more personal and authentic level. He became able to admit when he didn't know the answer to something. He was open about the challenges his company faced, but he also shared his confidence that he and his employees could navigate them together. He often said, "I don't know the answer to this question, but together we'll find the answer." He articulated and remained connected with his own sense of purpose, linked it to the company's, and helped his teams do the same. This lifted everyone's energy, and the sense of working together toward a clear common purpose boosted pride and cohesion within the company. He became a human leader who successfully steered employees and the company through the worst of the COVID crisis and its economic fallout. When he was promoted to become the CEO of an even larger company, news of his departure led to an outpouring of gratitude and well wishes from employees, which touched him deeply. He later adopted the same leadership approach in his new company with equal success.

What about Claire, who'd repressed part of herself to better fit her parents' vision of success? Once better aligned with who she was, she gave herself permission to tap fully into her emotional intelligence and hidden creative talents. She discovered that empathy came to her very naturally and easily, and she enjoyed connecting with people on a very human level, which made them feel heard, understood, and safe. Propelled with renewed energy and drive, she built and fired up a cohesive team, and with them, fulfilled with gusto the challenging role she'd been given. She flourished in her new company, gaining acceptance and respect both within and outside her organization.

David, whose combative and untrusting attitude had been shaped by his parents' and grandparents' World War II experiences, stopped fighting with the world and instead deployed his energy building strong connections within his team and with his peers, which greatly leveraged his impact.

Ray built a fulfilling new life after being pushed to retire from the company he'd been leading: he built a successful consulting practice and wrote a book to advocate for a cause close to his heart. On the back of the visibility and platform the book gave him, he was asked to head a nonprofit in that sphere, through which he greatly leveraged the impact he wanted to have. Being able to give back in that way, while spending more time with his family, gave him a sense of unprecedented joy, balance, and accomplishment.

After parting ways with his business partner, Blake mobilized his team behind his innovative vision for the business he'd created in the workspace sector. He hired collaborators aligned with his values and vision. Freed from self-doubt, he was able to fully unleash his own creativity and communicate far more clearly what he wanted to create and why, which focused and fired up his team. This collective energy and clear purpose have underpinned the company's success. He subsequently started a second company, where he deployed the same values and leadership approach.

Andrew, Claire, Chris, Ray, and Blake are not exceptions. When I ask people who've embarked on the journey to become human leaders what difference it has made in their lives, they echo similar sentiments: "It's life changing!" or "It's a revolution!" I see them energized and lighter, an invisible weight lifted from their shoulders. I notice the spring in their step. I see an inner flame ignite and radiate outwards, as their mindsets align with who they are and they experience the power of empathy. And I see them find meaning in doing something bigger than themselves and making a difference in other people's lives, starting with their immediate team. Like the child in this book's fable, they have found their own path of roses and they have unlocked their human gift. And like the child's, their journey has also been, and continues to be, one of learning and self-discovery.

In the introduction to this book, we talked about superhero leaders who approach their role as being infallible, unflappable, and fearless. These are not true heroes, however; like the magnificent statue in the Bible story, they look powerful and indomitable, but their head of gold rests on feet of clay. Identifying your mindtrap, deciding to shift it out of the way, and then embracing a mindbuild, however, makes you what writer Joseph Campbell defines as a hero: someone who embarks on a journey into the unknown, where they successfully overcome obstacles, before coming home transformed by the experience. But what then? What does this mean for the rest of the world? "The hero," Campbell writes, "comes back from this mysterious adventure with the power to bestow boons on his fellow man."[1] As such, becoming a human leader is precisely the kind of transformative adventure that makes those who undertake it the heroes whom Campbell is talking about. True heroes are those who dare to leave their comfort zone to embark on a very human journey and learn along the way. They also dare to embark on a journey with no end, for life keeps unfolding, and each day is an opportunity to grow and evolve. They are not afraid of change; in fact, they embrace it. Neither are they afraid of their own and others' humanity; they treasure it. This is how they become the best possible version of themselves and make their mark.

Human leaders also find meaning and immense satisfaction in working toward something bigger than themselves. This mindtrap-mindshift-mindbuild journey, besides changing the lives of leaders themselves, also makes a profound and lasting difference in the lives of people around them and the organizations they lead. Only leaders aligned with their own humanity are willing and able to discern other people's unique potential, understand what drives each one of them, and both unleash and channel this potential and drive toward a common purpose. Not only are they willing and able to do so but also helping others grow and transforming individual potential into collective power gives them immense satisfaction. Like ripples on a pond, human leaders' empathy and emotional intelligence reverberate throughout and beyond their organizations. By first transforming themselves, they change how they lead people, who in turn affect the people around them—other employees within the organization, but also customers, suppliers, shareholders, and entire communities. This is the extraordinary power of empathy, which leads to surprising results.

The ripples extend even further. Human leadership doesn't start and stop at the office: it happens everywhere and in each moment. It also happens at home, and those who've embarked on the journey can attest to the enormous difference it has made in their personal life. Leadership happens in the wider world, too. Addressing today's challenges, from economic crisis and social fractures to health and environmental threats, requires a different kind of leadership—what the World Economic Forum labels *governance 4.0*. It is what separates yesterday's leaders from those who can successfully navigate today's and tomorrow's challenges. This is how human leaders shine their light in the world: by changing the way they connect with themselves and other people, they start a chain reaction, because we are all part of interconnected networks of human relationships. Empathy is contagious, and because leaders set the tone and have more leverage, they are in a privileged position to make a difference.

So, as my grandmother once advised, *go now!* Go walk on your path of roses and unlock your human gift to make the impossible possible. Free your inner human leader and go shine your light brighter in the world.

Notes

Introduction

1. Norwest Venture Partners, "2018 Norwest CEO Journey Study." **https://www.nvp.com/ceojourneystudy/index.html#title**
2. Erica Goode, "Arnold Hutschnecker, 102, Therapist to Nixon," *New York Times*, January 3, 2001. **https://www.nytimes.com/ 2001/01/03/us/arnold-hutschnecker-102-therapist-to-nixon.html**
3. John Dowdy and Kirk Rieckhoff, "Agility in US National Security," McKinsey, March 2, 2017. Excerpt from *America's National Security Architecture: Rebuilding the Foundation* (Aspen Strategy Group, November 2016). **https://www.mckinsey.com/indus tries/public-and-social-sector/our-insights/agility-in-us-national-security**
4. Jim Harter, "Percent Who Feel Employer Cares About Their Wellbeing Plummets," Gallup, March 18, 2022. **https://www .gallup.com/workplace/390776/percent-feel-employer-cares-wellbeing-plummets.aspx**
5. Kim Peters and S. Alexander Aslam, "I Follow, Therefore I Lead: A Longitudinal Study of Leader and Follower Identity and Leadership in the Marines," *British Journal of Psychology* 109, no. 4, May 2018, pp. 708–723. **https://bpspsychub.onlinelibrary.wiley .com/doi/abs/10.1111/bjop.12312**
6. Mary Barra's commencement speech, the Stanford Graduate School of Business, 2016. **https://www.gsb.stanford.edu/insights/ mary-barra-what-every-b-school-graduate-should-know**
7. Geoff Colvin, *Humans Are Underrated: What High Achievers Know That Brilliant Machines Never Will* (Portfolio, 2015), p. 72.
8. Your Brain at Work podcast, "Compassion Wins at War and in the Office," transcript, Neuroleadership Institute, November 20, 2021. **https://your-brain-at-work.simplecast.com/episodes/ compassion-wins-at-war-and-in-the-office-BLV5IXfA/ transcript**
9. Author's interview with Marshall Goldsmith.
10. All my clients' names and some identifying details have been changed to protect their privacy.

Chapter 1

1. Scott Gleeson and Erik Brady, "When Athletes Share Their Battles with Mental Illness," *USA Today*, August 30, 2017. **https://www.usatoday.com/story/sports/2017/08/30/michael-phelps-brandon-marshall-mental-health-battles-royce-white-jerry-west/596857001/**

2. Kevin Love, "Everyone Is Going Through Something," *The Players' Tribune*, March 6, 2018. **https://www.theplayerstribune.com/articles/kevin-love-everyone-is-going-through-something**

3. Marshall Goldsmith, "20 Behaviors Even the Most Successful People Need to Stop," MG Thinkers 50 blog, October 26, 2015. **https://marshallgoldsmith.com/articles/teaching-leaders-what-to-stop/**

4. Sally Hegelsen and Marshall Goldsmith, *How Women Rise: Break the 12 Habits Holding You Back from Your Next Raise, Promotion, or Job* (New York: Hachette Books, 2018).

5. Tasha Eurich, *Insight: The Surprising Truth About How Others See Us, How We See Ourselves, and Why the Answers Matter More Than We Think* (Currency, 2017), p. 7.

6. Jonathan Levy, Abraham Goldstein, and Ruth Feldman, "The Neural Development of Empathy Is Sensitive to Caregiving and Early Trauma," *Nature* 10, article 1905, April 23, 2019. **https://www.nature.com/articles/s41467–019–09927-y**

7. Rianne Kok et al., "Normal Variation in Normal Parental Sensitivity Predicts Structural Brain Development," *Journal of the American Academy of Child and Adolescent Psychiatry* 54, no. 10, August 3, 2015, pp. 824–831. **https://www.jaacap.org/article/S0890–8567(15)00486–4/fulltext**

Chapter 2

1. Bessel van der Kolk, *The Body Keeps the Score: Brain, Mind, and Body in the Healing of Trauma* (New York: Penguin, 2014), chapter 4.

2. Katharine A. Kaplan, "College Faces Mental Health Crisis," *The Harvard Crimson*, January 12, 2004. **https://www.thecrimson.com/article/2004/1/12/college-faces-mental-health-crisis-one/**

3. John L. Oliffe, Brian Rasmussen, Joan L. Bottorff, Mary T. Kelly, Paul M. Galdas, Alison Phinney, and John S. Ogrodniczuk, "Masculinities, Work, and Retirement Among Older Men Who Experience Depression," *Qualitative Health Research Journal* 23, no. 12, December 1, 2013, pp. 1626–1637. **https://journals.sagepub.com/doi/abs/10.1177/1049732313509408**
4. BBC News, "Cameron Diaz to 'Un-Retire' from Acting with Jamie Foxx Film," June 30, 2022. **https://www.bbc.com/news/entertainment-arts-61992214**
5. Chris Cason, "Pau Gasol Discusses Four-Part Docuseries That Chronicles His Basketball Swan Song," *Forbes*, November 8, 2021. **https://www.forbes.com/sites/chriscason/2021/11/08/pau-gasol-discusses-four-part-docuseries-that-chronicles-his-swan-song-to-basketball/?sh=763ca7b54a37**
6. Alice Park, "Michael Phelps Opens Up About Retirement and Mental Health Awareness: 'I Struggle Through Problems Just Like Everybody Else,'" *Time Magazine*. Davos 2020 Mental Health. **https://time.com/collection/davos-2020-mental-health/5402066/michael-phelps-mental-health-activism/**
7. Dorie Clark and Christie Smith, "Help Your Employees Be Themselves at Work," *Harvard Business Review*, November 3, 2014. **https://hbr.org/2014/11/help-your-employees-be-themselves-at-work**

Chapter 3

1. Marshall Goldsmith and Mark Reiter, *The Earned Life: Lose Regret, Choose Fulfillment* (Currency, 2022), p. 16.
2. David M. Barnes and Ilan H. Meyer, "Religious Affiliation, Internalized Homophobia, and Mental Health in Lesbians, Gay Men, and Bisexuals," *American Journal of Orthopsychiatry* 82, no. 4, October 2012, pp. 505–515. **https://doi.org/10.1111/j.1939-0025.2012.01185.x**
3. Kevin Love, "Everyone Is Going Through Something," *The Players' Tribune*, March 6, 2018. **https://www.theplayerstribune.com/articles/kevin-love-everyone-is-going-through-something**
4. Joseph Campbell, "The Tigers and the Goats," *Myths of Light: Eastern Metaphors of the Eternal* (New York: Joseph Campbell Foundation, 2003).

5. Barbara Maranzani, "What Abraham Lincoln Was Carrying in His Pockets the Night He Was Killed," **Biography.com**, August 17, 2020. **https://www.biography.com/news/abraham-lincoln-pockets-assassination**

6. Ken Robinson with Lou Aronica, *The Element: How Finding Your Passion Changes Everything* (New York: Penguin, 2009), pp. 141–142.

7. Marshall Goldsmith and Mark Reiter, *The Earned Life: Lose Regret, Choose Fulfillment*, p. 17.

Chapter 4

1. Jonathan Gottschall, *The Storytelling Animal: How Stories Make Us Human* (Boston: Mariner Books, 2012).

2. Fritz Heider and Marianne Simmel, "An Experimental Study of Apparent Behavior," *The American Journal of Psychology* 57, no. 2, April 1944, pp. 243–259. **https://www.jstor.org/stable/1416950 ?origin=crossref**

3. V. S. Ramachandran, "The Neurons That Shaped Civilization," TEDIndia, November 2009. **https://www.ted.com/talks/vilaya nur_ramachandran_the_neurons_that_shaped_civilization**

4. Timothy D. Wilson, *Strangers to Ourselves: Discovering the Adaptive Unconscious* (Boston: Harvard University Press, 2004), p. 24. **https://www.youtube.com/watch?v=vJG698U2Mvo**

5. Daniel Simons and Christopher Chabris, "Selective Attention Test," 1999. **https://www.youtube.com/watch?v=vJG698U2Mvo**

6. Steve Jobs, 2005 Stanford commencement address. **https://news .stanford.edu/2005/06/14/jobs-061505/**

7. Michael Gross, *Genuine Authentic: The Real Life of Ralph Lauren* (New York: HarperCollins, 2003), p. 59.

8. Janine Willis and Alexander Todorov, "First Impressions: Making Up Your Mind After a 100-Ms Exposure to a Face," *Psychological Science* 17, no. 7, July 1, 2006. **https://journals.sagepub.com/ doi/10.1111/j.1467–9280.2006.01750.x**

9. William Ickes, "Empathic Accuracy: Judging Thoughts and Feelings," in Judith A. Hall, Marianne Schmid Mast, and Tessa V. West (Eds.), *The Social Psychology of Perceiving Others Accurately* (Cambridge, UK: Cambridge University Press, 2016). **https://www .researchgate.net/publication/273202952_Empathic_ accuracy_Judging_thoughts_and_feelings**

10. V. S. Ramachandran, "The Neurons That Shaped Civilization."

11. Greg J. Stephens, Lauren J. Silbert, and Uri Hasson, "Speaker-Listener Neural Coupling Underlies Successful Communication," *PNAS* 107, no. 32, July 26, 2010. **https://www.pnas.org/doi/10.1073/pnas.1008662107**

12. Mikkel Wallentin et al. "Amygdala and Heart Rate Variability Responses from Listening to Emotionally Intense Parts of a Story," *Neuroimage* 58, no. 3, October 1, 2011, 963–973. **https://pubmed.ncbi.nlm.nih.gov/21749924/**

13. Edward Schiappa et al., "Can One TV Show Make a Difference? Will and Grace and the Parasocial Contact Hypothesis," *Journal of Homosexuality* 21, no. 4, 2006. **https://pubmed.ncbi.nlm.nih.gov/17135126/**

14. Joe Holley, "Vanguard Mathematician George Dantzig Dies," *Washington Post*, May 19, 2005. **https://supernet.isenberg.umass.edu/photos/gdobit.html**

Chapter 5

1. Dare to Lead with Brené Brown, Spotify podcast, "Brené with Doug Conant on Finding and Telling Your Leadership Story," May 2021. **https://open.spotify.com/episode/30elYlQiSV03LUiU5mzFwF?go=1&sp_cid=a3da314090ebb1f61409d7d3e899a37f&utm_source=embed_player_v&utm_medium=desktop&nd=1**

2. Kevin Love, "Everyone Is Going Through Something," *The Players' Tribune*, March 6, 2018. **https://www.theplayerstribune.com/articles/kevin-love-everyone-is-going-through-something**

3. Atul Gawande, "Personal Best," *The New Yorker*, October 3, 2011. **https://www.newyorker.com/magazine/2011/10/03/personal-best**

4. Apple TV, "The Brazilian Storm," *Make or Break*, April 29, 2022, episode 3.

5. Bloomberg Markets and Finance, Interview with Satya Nadella, October 25, 2017. **https://www.youtube.com/watch?v=SbAPmVoWVZs**

6. The Henry Ford, "The Vagabonds." **https://www.thehenryford.org/collections-and-research/digital-resources/popular-topics/the-vagabonds**

7. Louann Brizendine, *The Female Brain* (New York: Broadway Books, 2006).
8. Dare to Lead with Brené Brown.
9. Eric Schmidt, Jonathan Rosenberg, and Alan Eagle, *Trillion Dollar Coach: The Leadership Playbook of Silicon Valley's Bill Campbell* (New York: Harper Business, 2019), p. 159.
10. "Why Men Are Lonelier in America Than Elsewhere," *The Economist*, January 1, 2022. **https://www.economist.com/united-states/2022/01/01/why-men-are-lonelier-in-america-than-elsewhere**
11. Bill George, "My Defining Moment," September 15, 2009. **https://www.billgeorge.org/page/my-defining-moment/**
12. Alan Mulally, "Working Together Webinar with Alan Mulally and Marshall Goldsmith," November 23, 2020. **https://www.youtube.com/watch?v=vYWMBhbLggA**

Chapter 7

1. Susan Jeffers, *Feel the Fear . . . and Do It Anyway* (Santa Monica, CA: Jeffers Press, 2007).
2. Emma Carmichael, "The Glorious Age of Adele," *Elle*, August 15, 2022. **https://www.elle.com/culture/music/a40803238/adele-interview-elle-september-cover-2022/**
3. A. S. Dalal, *Powers Within: Selections from the Works of Sri Aurobindo and the Mother* (Pondicherry: Sri Aurobindo Ashram), pp. 62–64.
4. Eileen and John Donahoe, "We Leaned into Our Marriage," Lean In, July 15, 2013. **https://leanin.org/news-inspiration/we-leaned-into-our-marriage**

Chapter 8

1. David R. Hawkins, *Power vs. Force: The Hidden Determinants of Human Behavior* (Carlsbad, CA: Hay House, 2014), chapter 4.
2. Bessel van der Kolk, *The Body Keeps the Score: Brain, Mind and Body in the Healing of Trauma* (New York: Viking, 2014), p. 343.
3. Sydney Rosen, *My Voice Will Go with You: The Teaching Tales of Milton H. Erickson* (New York: Norton, 1991), p. 46.

Chapter 9

1. Author's interview with Gail Miller.
2. Bronnie Ware, *Top Five Regrets of the Dying: A Life Transformed by the Dearly Departing* (Carlsbad, CA: Hay House, 2019).
3. Susan Kelly, "Woulda, Shoulda, Coulda: The Haunting Regret of Failing Our Ideal Selves," *Cornell Chronicle*, May 24 2018. **https:// news.cornell.edu/stories/2018/05/woulda-coulda-shoulda- haunting-regret-failing-our-ideal-selves**
4. HBO, "Very Ralph," 2019.
5. Stephen Hawking, *Brief Answers to the Big Questions* (New York: Bantam Books, 2018), p. 7.
6. Hubert Joly with Caroline Lambert, *The Heart of Business: Leader- ship Principles for the Next Era of Capitalism* (Harvard Business Review Press, 2021), p. 29. Hubert Joly is my husband.
7. Bill George, *Discover Your True North* (Hoboken, NJ: Wiley, 2015).
8. Hortense le Gentil, *Aligned: Connecting Your True Self with the Leader You're Meant to Be* (Vancouver: Page Two Books, 2019).
9. Sri Aurobindo, *Thoughts and Glimpses* (Aurobindo Ashram, 1973), p. 24.
10. Cited in Ellert Nijenhuis, *The Trinity of Trauma: Ignorance, Fragil- ity, and Control* (Göttingen: Vandenhoeck & Ruprecht, 2017), p. 181.
11. Ayse Birsel, *Design the Life You Love: A Step-by-Step Guide to Build- ing a Meaningful Future* (Berkeley: Ten Speed Press, 2015).
12. Hortense le Gentil's interview with Marshall Goldsmith.
13. Matthew McConaughey's Best Actor Academy Award acceptance speech, 2014. **https://www.youtube.com/watch?v=wD2cVhC- 63I**
14. Jane McGonigal, *Imaginable: How to See the Future Coming and Feel Ready for Anything—Even Things that Seem Impossible Today* (New York: Spiegel & Grau, 2022), p. 14.
15. Jane McGonigal, *Imaginable*, p. 75.
16. Jane McGonigal, *Imaginable*, p. 77.

Chapter 10

1. Jim Collins and Morten T. Hansen, "Great by Choice: How to Manage Through Chaos," *Fortune*, October 2011. **https://www .jimcollins.com/article_topics/articles/how-to-manage- through-chaos.html#articletop**

2. Lane Florsheim, "The Surprising Way Nike CEO John Donahoe Starts His Day," *Wall Street Journal*, August 30, 2021. **https:// www.wsj.com/articles/the-surprising-way-nike-ceo-john-donahoe-starts-his-day-11630326553**
3. My Morning Routine, "Arianna Huffington." **https://mymornin groutine.com/arianna-huffington/**
4. Greymatter podcast, "Eric Yuan: How Zoom Made Video the Pandemic Star," transcript, Greylock Partners, January 12, 2022. **https://greylock.com/greymatter/zoom-eric-yuan-full-screen-ahead/**
5. Madhuleena Roy Chowdhury, "The Neuroscience of Gratitude and Effects on the Brain," *Positive Psychology*, 9, April 2019. **https://positivepsychology.com/neuroscience-of-gratitude/ #neuroscience**
6. Adrian Gostick and Chester Elton, *Leading with Gratitude: Eight Leadership Practices for Extraordinary Business Results* (New York: Harper Business, 2020).
7. Kelly McGonigal, "How to Overcome Stress by Seeing Other People's Joy," *Greater Good Magazine*, July 5, 2017. **https:// greatergood.berkeley.edu/article/item/how_to_overcome_ stress_by_seeing_other_peoples_joy**
8. Martha M. Jablow, "Compassion Fatigue: The Toll of Being a Care Provider," American Association of Medical Colleges, July 11, 2017. **https://www.aamc.org/news-insights/compassion-fatigue-toll-being-care-provider**

Chapter 11

1. Michael Bungay Stanier, *The Coaching Habit: Say Less, Ask More & Change the Way You Lead Forever* (Vancouver: Page Two Books, 2016).
2. Hubert Joly with Caroline Lambert, *The Heart of Business: Leadership Principles for the Next Era of Capitalism* (Harvard Business Review Press, 2021), p. 40.
3. Author's interview with Hubert Joly.
4. David Remnick, "A Unified Field Theory of Bob Dylan," *The New Yorker*, October 24, 2022. **https://www.newyorker.com/ magazine/2022/10/31/a-unified-field-theory-of-bob-dylan**

5. BBC News, "Microsoft's Nadella Sorry for Women's Pay Comments," October 10, 2014. **https://www.bbc.com/news/ business-29571754**

6. Microsoft News Center, "Satya Nadella Email to Employees: RE: Grace Hopper Conference," October 9, 2014. **https://news .microsoft.com/2014/10/09/satya-nadella-email-to-employees-re-grace-hopper-conference/**

7. Mary Barra's commencement speech to the Stanford Graduate School of Business, 2016. **https://www.gsb.stanford.edu/ insights/mary-barra-what-every-b-school-graduate-should-know**

8. How to Be a Better Human podcast, "How to Find Your Voice (with Greta Morgan)," July 18, 2022. **https://podcasts.apple.com/us/ podcast/how-to-be-a-better-human/id1544098624?i= 1000570286728**

9. Thich Nhat Hanh, "Loving Speech and Deep Listening [Transcript]," January 18, 2022. **https://plumvillage.app/loving-speech-and-deep-listening-transcript/**

10. Dian Land, "Study Shows Compassion Meditation Changes the Brain," University of Wisconsin-Madison, March 25, 2008. **https:// news.wisc.edu/study-shows-compassion-meditation-changes-the-brain/**

11. **https://www.thehorseinstitute.com**. Special thanks to Marie-Claude Stockl and Lissa Pohl for putting together and facilitating our workshop.

12. Matt Weinberger, "'The Whining Is Over': How Microsoft CEO Satya Nadella Showed His Executives Tough Love," *Business Insider*, September 26, 2017. **https://finance.yahoo.com/news/ whining-over-microsoft-ceo-satya-233243862.html**

13. Geoff Colvin, *Humans Are Underrated: What High Achievers Know That Brilliant Machines Never Will* (Portfolio, 2015), pp. 93–97.

14. Adrian Gostick and Chester Elton, *Leading with Gratitude: Eight Leadership Practices for Extraordinary Business Results* (New York: Harper Business, 2020).

15. Steve Denning, "How Empathy Helped Generate a $2 Trillion Company," *Forbes*, July 18, 2021. **https://www.forbes.com/sites/ stevedenning/2021/07/18/how-empathy-helped-generate-a-two-trillion-dollar-company/?sh=764ebd474ebc**

16. "How to Be Vulnerable at Work Without Spilling Everything, From Brené Brown," **Ideas.TED.com**, March 1, 2021. **https://ideas .ted.com/how-to-be-vulnerable-at-work-without-spilling- everything-from-brene-brown/**
17. Adam Grant, "The Fine Line Between Helpful and Harmful Authenticity," *New York Times*, April 10, 2020. **https://www .nytimes.com/2020/04/10/smarter-living/the-fine-line- between-helpful-and-harmful-authenticity.html**
18. "How to Be Vulnerable at Work Without Spilling Everything, From Brené Brown."

Conclusion

1. Joseph Campbell, *The Hero with a Thousand Faces* (3rd ed.) (New York: New World Library, 2008), p. 23.

About the Author

Hortense le Gentil is a global executive leadership coach, speaker, and author. She works with CEOs and other senior executives around the world in their journey from hero leader to human leader.

Le Gentil's executive coaching is informed by her 30 years in business, working across a number of industries, in large corporations, and as an entrepreneur. She works on and delivers executive leadership programs at various Fortune 500 companies.

She was a 2021 nominee of the Thinkers 50 Coaching and Mentoring Awards. She is a contributor to *Harvard Business Review* and ThriveGlobal.com. Her thought leadership has been featured in *Forbes*, *Fast Company*, and *Business Insider*.

Her first book was titled *Aligned: Connecting Your True Self with the Leader You're Meant to Be.*

Writing collaborator **Caroline Lambert** has helped a wide range of changemakers and thought leaders in business, civil society, and politics translate their ideas and experience into books. Past collaborations include Hortense le Gentil's first book, *Aligned*, and Hubert Joly's *The Heart of Business*, a *Wall Street Journal* bestseller.

Previously a foreign correspondent and Deputy Asia Editor at *The Economist*, Caroline wrote about business, economics, and politics in various parts of the world, earning the Diageo Africa Business Reporting Award and the Sanlam Award for Excellence in Financial Journalism. Caroline holds an MBA from INSEAD and an MA in international relations from the Johns Hopkins University's School of Advanced International Studies, where she was awarded the Groove Haines Award in International Policy. She is a former Visiting Fellow at the Center for Global Development.

Index

E

Eastern spirituality, introduction, 91
Eat, Pray, Love (Gilbert), 91
Edison, Thomas, 90
Einfühlung (Vischer), 79
Elton, Chester, 178, 196
Emancipation Proclamation,
    issuance, 60–61
Emotional batteries, recharging, 181
Emotional connection, reliance, 193
Emotional intelligence, 105, 106
Emotional stories, impact, 79
Emotional support system, 96
Emotions
    bouncing, 181
    brain control, 70
    challenge, 140
    connection, 192–193
        fear, 7–8, 33
    draining, 143
    externalization, 143
    high-energy emotions, 135
    low-energy emotions, 135
    mindtrap, association, 145
    recognition, 94–95
    release, 141
    sharing, 199–200
    shift, 152
    substitution, 137–138
Empathic joy, 179
Empathy
    brain, wiring, 191
    business imperative, 198–199
    confusion, absence, 193–194
    cultivation, 13, 190–194
    importance, 90
    listening/leveraging, 161
    meditation, focus, 191
    self-protection, impact, 180
    term, usage, 4–5
    usage, 149
Empire Strikes Back, The (movie), 62
Emptiness, feeling, 95
Energy
    absorption, 40
    deployment, 204
    draining, 143–144
Energy-sapping emotions, mindtrap
    (connection), 147
Engagement feedback, 24

Enlightenment, finding, 111
Environment
    assessment, 77
    deciphering/filtering/scanning, 75–76
Episodic future thinking (EFT), 167–168
Equine-assisted learning, 191
Erickson, Milton, 136–137, 164
Eulogy, writing, 105, 158–159
Eurich, Tasha, 27
Exercise, importance, 113
Existential crises, absence, 126
External perspective
    benefit, 96
    consideration, value, 90
    helpfulness, 92
    impact, 84, 86–98
    maintenance, 95
    sources, 90–91
External trigger, 84
External voice, relevance, 108–112

F

Facebook, 129
Facial expressions, cues, 76–77
Factories, closure, 112
Failure, fear, 8, 33
Fears, 152
    challenge, 119
    confidence, connection, 127
    manifestation, 7–8
    overcoming, 128–129
    responses, 143–144
    substitution, 144
    sum, 6–8
Federer, Roger, 86
Feedback
    disbelief, 19
    engagement feedback, 24
    expectation, 88–89
    listening, willingness/ability, 96–97
    process, 33–34
Feedforward (coaching practice), 200
Feelings, 140
    challenge, 137–138, 142
    display, avoidance, 6
    triggers, 142–143
Ferreira, Italo, 87
Fifth Element, The (movie), 70
Fight-in-flight mode, 196
Firestone, Harvey, 90